DANIEL PLOOF

LORD, I'M

tired

GOSPEL TRUTH FOR A RESTLESS
AND WEARY SOUL

Psalm51
PUBLISHING
GALLATIN, TENNESSEE

Lord, I'm Tired: Gospel Truth for a Restless and Weary Soul
Copyright © 2024 by Daniel Ploof

Psalm51
PUBLISHING

Library of Congress Control Number: 2024917843

ISBN: 978-1-7373673-7-6 (print)
ISBN: 978-1-7373673-8-3 (e-book)
ISBN: 978-1-7373673-9-0 (audio)

Cover Design: German Creative
Book Editor: Jada Ploof

DEDICATION

To all those struggling to make it through another day,
may your weary souls find rest in Christ alone.

"But you, O LORD, are a shield about me, my glory, and the lifter of my head. I cried aloud to the LORD, and he answered me from his holy hill. I lay down and slept; I woke again, for the LORD sustained me."

— Psalm 3:3–5

CONTENTS

FOREWORD

Pastoral Perspective

Trust me. You will be blessed and challenged when you read through, **"Lord, I'm Tired: Gospel Truth for a Restless and Weary Soul."** The title is fitting for it describes the ebb and flow of the life of a true Christ-follower.

I really didn't understand how hard life can be until my dad went to be with the Lord in November of 2022. My dad was and still is my hero, and to no longer have him physically present with our family was a huge hurdle that left me feeling worn out on the inside. Many of you know what I'm talking about when it comes to facing something similar. For you, maybe it's not the loss of a loved one. Rather, as Dan covers in the following chapters, it may be a battle with anxiety, fear, or a battle with nagging sin.

Dan's opening sentence in the "Introduction" captures exactly what I felt at the time, and perhaps what you've felt in your life during the valley of a crisis. He notes, "Whether we care to admit it, most of us are incredibly tired and struggling to find the silver-lining of God's grace and mercy amid trials... Trials have enveloped our life, stress has plagued our mind, and depression continues to knock at the door, waiting patiently for us to lower our guard and overwhelm our soul" (13).

Is there an easy fix to relieve us from the valley of suffering and weariness? Outside of having a saving relationship with the Lord Jesus, the answer is always a resounding, "NO!" There is help, however, and that comes through the One who loves us far more than we could ever imagine.

I applaud Dan for making the Gospel of the Lord Jesus clear in what he expresses in the twenty chapters before you. Dan declares, "Ephesians 2:8-9 clearly articulates how a person must be saved to enter the kingdom of heaven... Good works play no part in salvation, other than testifying to a changed heart sold out for Christ" (165).

Moreover, he does a masterful job of painting a course forward out of our weariness and the stressors of life by using God's Word, the Scriptures, as the compass that will lead us toward help for our weary souls. Dan points out, "Without the truth of Scripture to strengthen our faith and encourage our hearts, we will never return to center and recalibrate our truth north when we are hopelessly lost" (22).

Furthermore, I am happy to endorse Dan's book because He gets real with numerous feelings and experiences that not all Christian authors will be transparent about in their writings. In my Southern vernacular, he doesn't "beat around the bush" with what may be clandestinely tucked away in our lives. Sometimes, we may be tired and weary due to harboring sin. I love the fact that Dan calls this out, and he calls on us to repent of it and surrender everything in our life to the lordship of Jesus.

Even still, I love the way Dan points out that often the trials, suffering, or crises we face are used by God to help us draw closer to the Lord. I can now say, almost two years to the date that my dad went to be with the Lord, He has used my dad's passing to draw me closer to Himself. Thank you, Dan, for showing your readers that trials have a purpose. If we can come to see that with the Spirit's help, we will be further along in finding our way back to a place of peace and satisfaction in the Lord's good providence in our lives!

Finally, I can recommend this book to you because I have seen Dan's character lived out right in front of me. He's a good friend, and as his pastor, I've been able to see him pour into the lives of numerous men in our church. What he writes about in the following pages is what he seeks to live out in his own family and within his church family. Buckle up and get ready to be challenged and blessed!

Grace and peace,

Dr. Travis Fleming

Senior Pastor, First Baptist Church, Gallatin, TN

PREFACE

God's Sovereignty

When I reflect upon trials in my life, knowing God is in control comforts me. I have nothing to fear because His will for my life is sovereignly ordained. He has a purpose in mind for every hardship I encounter and His Word gives me peace. Therefore, I do not have to feel burdened knowing why He allows trials to test me. Rather, I can rest in the truth of Scripture which encourages me to trust His sovereignty with all my heart and without conditions.

"Lord, I'm Tired," is a glimpse into 20 issues I have wrestled with throughout my life. Each topic has consumed my mind and tempted me to question God's will when I could not make sense of it all. Even now, I struggle reconciling things God uses to mold my personal character. I am comforted knowing that despite my weaknesses, God is perfecting me. His Word reminds me that trials keep me dependent upon Him, so I will praise all the more because pain and hardship are often His way of drawing me closer to Him.

The Lord has been more gracious and merciful than I deserve, teaching me that freedom is attainable when I surrender to His authority, obey His Word, and submit to His sovereign will for my life. Therefore, my goal is to glorify Him by helping others discover the same rest He has given me. For joy and peace are found in Christ alone, and I want nothing more than to praise Him for all He has done by encouraging others to love His Word like I do.

Life does not always turn out the way we prefer. We cannot predict when pain, suffering, or calamity will rise up and steal our joy. That is why we must guard our hearts and minds before we enter seasons of trial to ensure we are well-prepared when our faith is tested. Oftentimes, we react to what the enemy throws our way rather than ensuring our spiritual armor is secure ahead of time. In that moment, the only thing which matters is whether we are disciplined to resist temptation and respond to the enemy's lies by the power of the Holy Spirit.

It is easy to assume we are ready for battle when we have trained well in advance. However, if our spiritual disciplines are lax and infrequent, what makes us think we can withstand the onslaught of spiritual weapons Satan has at his disposal? God's Word is the only weapon powerful enough to keep the enemy at bay, which means it must be our source of truth to identify a counterfeit when we see it. The enemy is sophisticated enough to twist God's Word against us. Therefore, we must know what Scripture teaches so we are not deceived when we are tired.

Whether suffering from physical, emotional, psychological, or spiritual fatigue, God is not absent in our time of need. He is standing in the fire with us. Jesus defeated sin and death on the cross of Calvary! Whom then shall we fear? Our Savior empathizes with our emotions because He walked a mile in our shoes. Thus, we can rest securely on the promises of Scripture because He died to set us free. The only question is whether we will trust His sovereignty or remain in bondage to the pleasures of this world which solve nothing but only enslave our minds further.

INTRODUCTION
Overwhelmed By Fatigue

Whether we care to admit it, most of us are incredibly tired and struggling to find the silver-lining of God's grace and mercy amid trials. We are physically, mentally, emotionally, and spiritually worn out, struggling to make it through another day. Trials have enveloped our life, stress has plagued our mind, and depression continues to knock at the door, waiting patiently for us to lower our guard and overwhelm our soul. How then should we respond? Can we truly gain victory over our troubles when we are overcome by fear and anxiety?

If we are honest, some of us have contemplated suicide, taking matters into our own hands as a viably foolish solution to our problems. Hopelessness and doubt have become a dysfunctional security blanket rather than the saving grace of God's Word. Rather than placing faith and trust in Jesus, we have lost sight of wisdom because quality time with the Lord has all but vanished from our daily priorities. Busyness has become our default, and we have no idea how to break the cycle and get off the hamster's wheel which leads nowhere and only wears us out.

We often feel overwhelmed by fatigue because we have allowed the enemy's lies to solely dwell upon our minds. As a result, we allow Satan to plant seeds of hopelessness in our hearts which only nurtures insecurities. No wonder we are tempted to run from our problems and isolate from others! We have lost all hope that our Father in heaven hears our cries and is willing to step in and save us.

However, the beauty of Scripture is that it casts light into the darkness of our mind, exposing false doctrine we have chosen to believe and pointing us to Christ as our source of wisdom and strength. Keep in mind, what makes God's Word so powerful is that it is absolute truth in which we can bind our hearts. We are nothing without Jesus, which is why it is hypercritical that we remain connected to Him at all times through the power of the Holy Spirit and Scripture (John 15:1-11).

"Whoever confesses that Jesus is the Son of God, God abides in him, and he in God. So we have come to know and to believe the love that God has for us. God is love, and whoever abides in love abides in God, and God abides in him."

— 1 John 4:15–16

Sadly, we often believe we need to shoulder our burdens and carry our cross on our own. In turn, we walk around bearing an eight-hundred-pound gorilla on our backs while complaining about how burdened and tired we feel. If only we would cast our cares upon Jesus, we would find rest for our weary souls and release the crushing weight of hopelessness and despair which tempts us to throw in the towel and give up altogether.

There is simply no justifiable reason for any of us to shoulder that burden. It only stunts our growth and restricts Gospel truth from entering our minds and flooding our hearts. That is why we must lay down our burdens of fatigue, anxiety, guilt, shame, and regret over our sins. Jesus promised that if we would exchange our burdens for His yoke of righteousness, which is easy and light (Matt. 11:28-30), He would provide contentment through grace and mercy which inevitably brings us peace.

"Peace I leave with you; my peace I give to you. Not as the world gives do I give to you. Let not your hearts be troubled, neither let them be afraid."

— John 14:27

Oftentimes, we view fatigue as something we should avoid like the plague, but that train of thought is man-focused, not God-centered. When we view being tired as a terrible thing, we miss out on blessings God has in store for those who recognize their depravity. God does not want us to feel enslaved to exhaustion. Rather, He wants us to sacrifice our fears at the foot of the cross and trust Him without reservation for our salvation.

Fatigue draws us closer to God, not farther away from Him. In this, we must consider hardship with Biblical perspective, knowing He has a sovereign plan and purpose for every trial we face. God is not immune to our cries for help but knows what we need. The greater question is whether we will trust His timing or give up hope. All we need to survive today and prepare for tomorrow is to give Him the benefit of the doubt, relinquish our pride, and accept that His will be done, come what may.

"For I will satisfy the weary soul, and every languishing soul I will replenish."

— Jeremiah 31:25

In the end, rest for our weary souls begins with conceding, **"Lord, I am tired!"** But it does not end there, because God has abundant wisdom to share if we open our hearts and trust His

Word. That is why the chapters of this book were written in a "prayer" format of personal struggle and prayer request to focus our minds on the things we cry out to God on a regular basis. Granted, it is not an exhaustive list but a starting point to relinquish the yoke of slavery we have held onto for far too long.

Therefore, let us embrace fatigue, knowing that weakness draws us closer to God. Let us also fix our eyes upon Jesus to discover the freedom our souls desperately crave. For the yoke He offers is easy because His burden is light, but we cannot allow fear, doubt, anxiety, and hopelessness to bait us into believing He is powerless to save. Instead, we must trust Him completely because He is all-powerful and can speak truth into the darkness of our souls to rescue us from bondage.

Our Father in heaven never guaranteed a life of comfort for us. Rather, He promised eternal rest to those who trust in the name of Jesus Christ for salvation. That means we must accept the hand we are dealt and count our trials as joy. Surely, pain and suffering will continue to torment our minds, but they enable us to praise God in our hardships as well. In the end, trials draw us closer to Christ, for which we must be thankful.

> *"The road to the Kingdom is not so pleasant, and comfortable, and easy, and flowery, as many dream. It is not a bright, sunny, flowery path. It is not paved with triumph, though it is to end in victory. The termination is glory, honor, and immortality; but on the way, there is the thorn in the flesh, the sackcloth, and the cross. Recompense later; but labor here! Rest later; but weariness here! Joy and security later; but here endurance and watchfulness — the race, the battle, the burden, the stumbling block, and oftentimes the heavy heart."*
>
> *— Horatius Bonar*
> *"The Surety's Cross," 1873.*

CHAPTER 1

Help! I Am Lost
(I'm tired of feeling all alone.)

Many of us love watching "survival" shows on television. There is something about attempting to conquer the wild outdoors which grabs our attention and captivates our minds. Contestants always assume they possess the physical skills and mental fortitude to survive alone in the wilderness. However, it does not take too long before hunger pangs set in, harsh elements batter the body, and mind games wreak havoc to make one thing abundantly clear. Nature always wins!

The rugged wilderness is unforgiving, ruthless, and relentless. Harsh weather conditions and predators make survival extremely difficult, yet that has not deterred adventure seekers from testing their personal abilities time and again. Humanity has never conquered nature. Nevertheless, countless men and women venture deep into the vast unknown for weeks, months, and even years on end with dreams of assessing their skills and resilience to survive, no matter what happens.

If we peel back the layers of our hearts, it becomes clear why so many of us continue to test our luck and venture deep into the wilderness. We feel lost and do not know who we are because we have fallen victim to an identity crisis. As a result, we set out on a spiritual voyage of sorts, like Jack Sparrow in search of buried treasure, hoping to discover our meaning and purpose in life by pushing our physical endurance to the limit and stretching our mind further than ever before.

> *"Now faith is the assurance of things hoped for, the conviction of things not seen."*
>
> — *Hebrews 11:1*

If we have ever watched the survival series, "Alone," on *The History Channel*®, some contestants admit defeat and give up entirely when they could continue on. Why? It was not because they lacked adequate shelter to protect themselves from inclement weather and dangerous predators. Neither was it because they lacked fresh drinking water, struggled to keep fire alive, or failed to find sustainable food sources to meet their physical needs. They gave up because hopelessness consumed their minds.

Isolation broke them to the point where they could not find a justifiable reason to go on. The physical pain was tolerable, but the reality of being cut off from civilization with no end in sight was too much to mentally bear. They believed the lie of isolation which told them they were all alone. Their attention was 100% focused on a lack of horizontal relationships with loved ones rather than vertical intimacy with God which they truly needed.

It is easy to get lost in the wilderness of our minds when we have removed ourselves from fellowship and community. The prophet, Elijah, suffered great hopelessness and despair when he isolated himself after experiencing countless miracles. Despite all God had done in and through him, Elijah fell into a deep depression because his focus was centered on humanity instead of the One who sovereignly provided him protection from harm.

"God has not rejected his people whom he foreknew. Do you not know what the Scripture says of Elijah, how he appeals to God against Israel? 'Lord, they have killed your prophets, they have demolished your altars, and I alone am left, and they seek my life.' But what is God's reply to him? 'I have kept for myself seven thousand men who have not bowed the knee to Baal.'"

— Romans 11:2–4

God did not allow Elijah to stay self-focused, reminding him not by works of power and majesty but in the silence of a quiet whisper that He was with him. Elijah simply needed to shift his perspective off what he lacked in personal relationships and find peace and contentment in the Lord. That is why isolation is so dangerous, because it cuts us off from accountability and baits us into thinking we are alone when nothing could be further from the truth. God is with us wherever we go, and He will not forsake us no matter how far we fall into the valley of despair.

Conventional wisdom says we can survive three days without fresh drinking water and three weeks without food, yet countless souls live without spiritual nourishment every day of their lives. They are content to starve themselves rather than turn to faith in Christ for survival. In this, they miss one critical fact. Since our souls are eternal, would we not be better served ensuring our faith is well-nourished rather than parched and empty? Is eternity not more important than our temporary, physical sufferings?

"And after you have suffered a little while, the God of all grace, who has called you to his eternal glory in Christ, will himself restore, confirm, strengthen, and establish you."

— 1 Peter 5:10

Regretfully, we choose death over life far too often when the solution to our problems is virtually within our grasp. We must open our hearts and tune our ears to the Father calling us home. The challenge is we are often spiritually blind to our own blindness and fail to recognize our malnourishment. We assume we are healthy, but that is a lie. Truly, we are no different than the scribes and Pharisees whom Jesus called "whitewashed tombs" because of their pride and self-deception.

The problem is we desperately want to prove our self-worth in this life and will exhaust every tool, skill, and survival method at our disposal to prove we can save ourselves rather than ask for help. It is a matter of pride if we are honest enough to admit it. However, if we would open our eyes for one second, we would realize that God is patiently standing before us with a lifeline in hand. He is ready and willing to not only meet our physical needs, but our spiritual need for salvation as well.

There is no justifiable reason to starve ourselves in search of greater fulfillment outside of Christ. Just as King Solomon sought to find purpose and meaning in the things of this world, we too must come to the same conclusion he did, that the Lord alone is our true source of spiritual fulfillment. That is why God gave us His Word to protect our minds. It is incredibly easy to justify sin as a self-protecting necessity if we are not bathing our minds in absolute truth. It distinguishes darkness from the light of Christ and calls us home to our heavenly Father where hope and healing are found.

"The end of the matter; all has been heard. Fear God and keep his commandments, for this is the whole duty of man. For God will bring every deed into judgment, with every secret thing, whether good or evil."

— Ecclesiastes 12:13–14

When we watch survival contestants on "Alone," we often see a shift in their perspective from pure joy in the newness of the experience to depression in the isolation of the wilderness. What once was exciting becomes mundane, monotonous, and exhausting without someone to share in the personal experience. Likely, few contestants considered how intense the mental anguish would be when they agreed to test their merit. However, time has a way of filtering out things in this world which matter from those we can truly live without.

"But godliness with contentment is great gain, for we brought nothing into the world, and we cannot take anything out of the world. But if we have food and clothing, with these we will be content."

— 1 Timothy 6:6–8

The challenge is we will never know what is most important in life if we are not grounded in the truth of Scripture for wisdom and discernment. Through its pages, we experience a personal relationship with our Creator because He reminds us of who we are, why we were made, and what our primary purpose should be in life. In other words, our true identity is found in Him rather than what the world teaches. We are never alone in Christ because He walks with us through the valley of the shadow of death (Psalm 23:4).

Most people who apply to be contestants on survival shows are drawn to the experience by fame, prize money, and financial endorsements. However, if we focus our attention on the interviews throughout each episode, we will find contestants looking to prove or accomplish something which money cannot buy. They are seeking answers to questions we all wrestle with this side of heaven. Who am I? Why was I made? What is my ultimate purpose in life?

God's Word answers all these questions and much more, for it is more than a crutch we lean on in times of trouble. It is life-giving nourishment straight from God's heart which sustains us through trials and tests our mental fortitude and spiritual maturity. Faith has the power to change our perspective if we are willing to relinquish control to God and allow Him to guide our paths. Yet to do so, we must relinquish pride and surrender our lives to His ultimate authority and sovereign will.

Virtually every tool or resource necessary for survival has a tangible purpose. Why wouldn't it? If we find ourselves in a survival scenario, we will need fire, shelter, fresh water, and food to live. However, do we ever stop and consider what we will need after those few days have elapsed? Do we have a plan of action for the future? What if we are cut off from human interaction? Are we prepared to endure mental anguish and spiritual warfare, or will we give up when isolation becomes unbearable?

The Bible may not be the first tool we consider packing in our bug out bag, but it is the most critical tool we need for long-term survival to find out who we are and what we are made of when we venture into the wilderness. Without the truth of Scripture to strengthen our faith and encourage our hearts, we will never return to center and recalibrate our true north when we are hopelessly lost. We will simply wander alone in the wilderness with no sense of direction and little chance of survival.

"One who wanders from the way of good sense will rest in the assembly of the dead."

— *Proverbs 21:16*

We can choose to surrender control to God. We can also equip ourselves for the journey ahead and ensure we are prepared to overcome the trials this world has to offer. We are not alone. God is with us and His Word is forever true, guiding our paths toward righteousness. Therefore, let us ground our faith in the truth of His Word which reminds us that this world is not our home. Heaven awaits and all we need to get there is the faith of a mustard seed to trust in Jesus and relinquish ultimate control of our lives to Him.

"So we do not lose heart. Though our outer self is wasting away, our inner self is being renewed day by day. For this light momentary affliction is preparing for us an eternal weight of glory beyond all comparison, as we look not to the things that are seen but to the things that are unseen. For the things that are seen are transient, but the things that are unseen are eternal."

— 2 Corinthians 4:16–18

Whether we are prone to isolate ourselves physically, emotionally, psychologically, or spiritually, feeling lost can be crippling. Many of us have fallen victim to hopelessness and depression because we felt alone. We assumed no one could relate to what we were thinking and feeling. So, we waved the white flag of surrender and allowed the enemy to wreak havoc in our minds. Granted, we never intended to throw in the towel and give up. It just happened when the walls began to close in around us.

The beauty of hitting rock bottom is that we have nowhere to go but up. When we have come to the point where we are sick and tired of being sick and tired, heart change begins to happen because we are willing to seek wise counsel and fresh perspective. God is capable of turning our ashes to beauty, but we must take the first step and allow His Spirit full access to our broken hearts. He will restore our joy, but first we must stop looking for satisfaction in worldly pleasures and turn to Christ for fulfillment instead.

Application

1. When have you been hopelessly lost? How did that make you feel? What did you learn as a result?

2. Why is it so dangerous to be spiritually lost?

3. Would you consider yourself well-nourished or malnourished in your knowledge and application of God's Word? Why?

4. How have you forgotten about what is most important in life by chasing after the pleasures of this world?

5. Do you know who you are, why God made you, and for what purpose? Why or why not?

6. What is your greatest tool for surviving the trials and tribulations of this world? How so?

7. Why does God meet us in the valley of despair rather than the mountaintop of peace, joy, and contentment?

Prayer

Lord, I am hopelessly lost at times. Despite my best efforts, my mind tends to drift off-course. I find myself all alone with no one to rely upon for salvation. Help me abandon my pride and admit my shortcomings so I can hear Your absolute truth ringing in my ears. The enemy continues to torment with lies, tempting me to lose hope that You can save me. That is why I numb my pain with worldly pleasures rather than seek Your Word for salvation. Help me remain patiently still so I can hear the Holy Spirit whispering truth to my soul, leading me home to the security of Your arms. I am tired of being lost, Lord. I surrender my life to You, unconditionally and without hesitation. Amen.

CHAPTER 2

Lord, Give Me Guidance
(Teach me to do Your will.)

How often do we ask for help? What causes us to rely upon our own strength when we know it is limited? Would it not make more sense to lean upon those who have greater wisdom, knowledge, and understanding? Oftentimes, we find ourselves swimming in an ocean of chaos, content with exhaustively treading water rather than accepting help from God. Why? Are we so consumed by trials, fears, and insecurities that we fail to recognize the lifeline He provides when we are sinking? Or, if we are being honest, do we even want help from God at all?

"Behold, I stand at the door and knock. If anyone hears my voice and opens the door, I will come into him and eat with him, and he with me."

— *Revelation 3:20*

What we must understand during seasons of trials is how deep roots of pride, arrogance, and stubbornness extend into our hearts. However, do we even recognize them? Perhaps we have turned so calloused towards accepting help that self-reliance has become a security blanket, despite its insufficiency. Thankfully,

Psalm 32:8 forces us to address the depth and breadth of how calloused we have become and whether we will accept help from the Lord. For if we continue leaning upon our own understanding, we will surely reap the consequences of our sins.

"I will instruct you and teach you in the way you should go; I will counsel you with my eye upon you."

— *Psalm 32:8*

There are basically two ways to learn a hard lesson. Heed the wisdom of others which aligns with the absolute truth of God's Word, or personally experience it for ourselves no matter what happens. Typically, we look inward because firsthand experience feels more tangible and trustworthy in the moment. We trust what we can physically sense, regardless of whether our personal judgment is legitimate or not. Yet what we fail to realize is how difficult the path toward wisdom can be when we reject wise counsel and rely upon our own understanding.

"The way of a fool is right in his own eyes, but a wise man listens to advice."

— *Proverbs 12:15*

Keep in mind, there are many justifiable reasons why we choose self-reliance rather than wise counsel. Perhaps there are no honest, discerning, or Biblically-sound followers of Christ present in our lives, who are equipped to answer our questions. It could be that we have no one trustworthy who has our best interest in mind when giving their opinion or is impartial enough to speak truth in love. What we need more than anything are Biblical counselors who will tell us what we need to hear vs. what we selfishly desire. However, that type of wise counsel can be difficult to find if we do not know anyone who is available to talk, Biblically grounded, and equipped to help us.

"Better is open rebuke than hidden love. Faithful are the wounds of a friend; profuse are the kisses of an enemy."

— Proverbs 27:5–6

Conversely, perhaps we have been misled, either intentionally or unintentionally, and hurt by the counsel of others. How then do we cope? Most of us choose to self-protect by leaning upon personal strength, even though our knowledge is limited and our perspective is biased. Therefore, self-reliance may not always be the wisest option to choose. Nevertheless, trusting ourselves is typically the predominant path we take when trials arise, because it is comfortable, logical, and familiar.

Since the fall of Adam, personal experience has always been the path of least resistance as we do not have to filter our thoughts through God or even second opinions. We simply react or respond based on our best, educated guess and deal with consequences as they come to fruition. The problem is when we rely upon ourselves rather than wise, Biblical counsel, we tend to isolate from those who can help us or disregard that we need any help at all, especially from God and His Word.

When I reflect upon my transition from bachelorhood to marriage, I realize that it took me a while to break away from a singleness mentality and lean upon my wife for input and advice. I was so used to making independent decisions that I closed myself off from her accountability. I failed miserably at including her in the discernment process while making important decisions for our family. Foolishly, I bypassed her thoughts and opinions without realizing how I was causing division in our marriage.

Once I recognized how irrational it was to isolate myself from her, we became a more united couple.

Isolation is a slippery slope toward self-deception because accountability is non-existent in a relationship of one. Thus, if we desire to know the wisest path when faced with tough decisions, we must relinquish control and allow others who fear the Lord and obey His commands to speak truth into our lives. However, whose voice do we typically allow to influence our decision-making? Moreover, are the trusted advisors we depend upon to speak wisdom into our hearts willing to be held accountable by God for their counsel to us?

Trusting the Lord is difficult for most people, Christians included. It may seem easy on the surface, but when the storms of life overwhelm our minds, we tend to shift gears and default into self-protection mode without thinking about it. In many cases, trials which seem within our control to influence require greater faith to relinquish. As a result, if there is something we have the power to change, we will instinctively react based on personal knowledge and rely upon firsthand experience.

However, if we know we have absolutely no strength, power, or authority to influence trials and tribulations, trust seems much easier to embrace. The greater the trial, the easier to relinquish control. For example, natural disasters and terminal illnesses are areas of grave concern which we have no power to stop from happening. Therefore, it should be easier to trust the Lord for courage, strength, wisdom, discernment, and understanding in those moments, not harder. Easier said than done, though, when the storms of life come crashing upon us!

"For thus says the LORD, who created the heavens (he is God!), who formed the earth and made it (he established it; he did not create it empty, he formed it to be inhabited!): 'I am the LORD, and there is no other. I

did not speak in secret, in a land of darkness; I did not say to the offspring of Jacob, "Seek me in vain." I the LORD speak the truth; I declare what is right."'

— Isaiah 45:18–19

For example, when my mother was dying from cancer many years ago, I felt incredible peace during the storm of her terminal illness. Trusting God amid the pain and confusion was effortless. I knew the only one who could save her was the Lord, not her doctors, treatments, or medications. Her life was precious, and in His sovereignty He held the power to temporarily heal her body (which He did not) or call her home to eternity in heaven (which He did over twenty years ago).

That is not to say accepting my mother's death was easy. I mourned her loss greatly, but trusting God made the process much easier to reconcile, not harder. Oftentimes, we cannot comprehend God's sovereignty in the moment because we fail to see the big picture. We lack hindsight perspective to make sense of it all. However, Jesus taught His disciples an important lesson during His ministry. That being, the trials we face have greater purpose for the kingdom than we could ever imagine. That is why we must trust Him instead of relying on ourselves for strength.

It takes great humility to admit we do not have all the answers. Many of us put up a good front publicly and act as if we have life under control. However, behind closed doors we are struggling to survive and coping with the trials of life as best we can. How then do we overcome pride, arrogance, and insecurities, and humble ourselves by asking the Lord for help? Is He not fully capable of guiding our steps? He is the omniscient Creator of the universe. Do we genuinely think we know better than Him, or are we simply too scared to ask for His help?

"When pride comes, then comes disgrace, but with the humble is wisdom."

— *Proverbs 11:2*

There is no shame admitting we do not know everything, because something deep inside us desires to know what is right, wrong, good, and evil. For example, curiosity and selfishness drove the desire within Eve to eat from the tree of knowledge in the garden of Eden. It likewise motivates us each time we lean on our own understanding rather than yield to God's sovereign omniscience. Deep down, we desire to pull ourselves up by our bootstraps and prove we are self-sufficient, but what purpose does that serve? Why would we pridefully maintain independence from God rather than depending upon Him for wisdom?

That is why Psalm 32:8 is such an encouraging promise we cannot ignore or disregard, for God has taken it upon Himself to personally teach us the wisest path we must take in life. There is a reason He preserved His Word for thousands of years, and we must understand that absolute truth never returns void. If we open our Bibles and study its precepts daily, God's will is easy to distinguish because we are willing to listen, obey, and apply what we're reading. The Lord blesses teachable hearts with wisdom, which requires us to humble ourselves daily.

The real question is whether we want to hear what He has to say in the first place. I admit I have quickly skimmed over many Bible verses which speak directly to my struggles. Granted, it is not that I did not want to hear the Lord's voice speaking directly to my issues or failed to value what Scripture teaches. Regrettably, I do not always want to filter my life through the lens of Scripture because truth is convicting and exposes my insecurities and failures. That is why I often hide in the shadows rather than own my sins and the consequences of my actions.

My problems derive more from selfish desires being at the center of my life rather than Jesus Christ. No wonder I have been far more discontent and hopelessly lost than I care to admit! Far too often, I lose track of who is most important and substitute God's provision for self-sufficiency. Sadly, I believe I often know better. Therefore, receiving proper guidance and discernment from the Lord are all about humbling myself daily and seeking ample opportunities to practice what I preach. I simply cannot avoid the conviction of the Holy Spirit altogether and foolishly do things my own way without severe consequences.

"For I know the plans I have for you, declares the LORD, plans for welfare and not for evil, to give you a future and a hope. Then you will call upon me and come and pray to me, and I will hear you. You will seek me and find me when you seek me with all your heart."

— Jeremiah 29:11–13

Undoubtedly, trust and humility are a package deal, for we will never learn what God has in store for us if we do not humble ourselves, admit our failures and deficiencies, and trust the all-sufficiency of His Word as divinely inspired, absolute truth. Truly, the Lord is not interested in halfhearted attempts to yield our personal will if we are flippantly disinterested in obeying His commands. Rather, He wants us to trust Him wholeheartedly without doubt, hesitation, expectations, or conditions. Only then will we find rest for our tired and weary souls.

"And those who know your name put their trust in you, for you, O LORD, have not forsaken those who seek you."

— Psalm 9:10

That is one reason many intellectuals struggle embracing true Christianity, because they are unwilling to place faith in the triune God of holy Scripture. They struggle reconciling that there is an absolute standard of righteousness and morality in this world. So, they reject the Bible entirely and seek to discredit its validity rather than consider and embrace its inerrancy. As a result, they hedge their bets on preconceived notions and reject Scripture altogether, not realizing how critical eternal salvation is to survival this side of heaven.

It takes an immeasurable amount of pride and arrogance to assume we know better than God. History is full of brilliant men and women who were unwilling to trust the Gospel of salvation through Jesus Christ and died as proud, self-justified atheists. Today, those unfortunate souls are languishing in hell because they chose to reject God and disregard the warnings of holy Scripture. They were too prideful to surrender to God's authority, obey His Word, and submit to His sovereign will. Now they are suffering eternal anguish and torment because of their unbelief in the Gospel of Jesus Christ.

"There is a way that seems right to a man, but its end is the way to death."

— Proverbs 16:25

Whether or not we believe the Bible is true, it is unapologetic in its position as the ultimate authority and standard of righteousness we are expected to follow. Therefore, do we believe God's Word is true (yesterday, today, and tomorrow)? Are we resolute that His Word is inerrant cover-to-cover? Will we cling to it as our guiding light toward righteousness and peace? It is the ultimate question we must reconcile in our lives and the determining factor whether we will enter heaven one day or not.

Keep in mind, if God is who He says He is in the pages of Scripture, and if He truly sacrificed His Son to ransom our souls from the grips of hell, we must respond in faith and accept that His Word is the only standard of truth by which we will live. No matter what our culture teaches, there is no other viable option to forgive our sins and save our souls. That means we have a critical choice to make which will determine our fate. If we choose Christ, we are ensured eternity in heaven. If we choose the alternative, we are destined to spend eternity in hell.

"Jesus said to him, 'I am the way, and the truth, and the life. No one comes to the Father except through me.'"

— John 14:6

Granted, salvation demands unconditional trust and requires us to humble ourselves daily. However, the more we relinquish control to God and seek His Word for wisdom and discernment, the easier it will become to create healthy, spiritual disciplines which will aid us in the future. It all comes down to the attitude and posture of our hearts. The more we feed on the bounty of God's Word, the more we will discover our purpose in life and begin living for a higher calling.

That is our plight as followers of Jesus Christ and we must embrace it wholeheartedly and without hesitation to the honor and glory of His precious name. Not to say that trusting God is effortless, but it is made easier when we reflect upon all Christ has done for us and respond by faith in gratitude for the gift He graciously bestowed on us. Our Savior did not have to die in our place. Rather, He chose to sacrifice Himself because He loves us, and we are wise to never forget how lost we would truly be if He had not saved our souls from self-destruction.

Application

1. Do you struggle asking for help? Why or why not?

2. Who do you typically ask for wisdom and counsel? Whose voice reigns supreme in your life?

3. Where would the Bible rank in the list of resources you turn to during seasons of trial?

4. Why does self-reliance feel like a safer bet than asking others for help?

5. Why does God want you to trust Him, first and foremost, when you need guidance?

6. How can you use God's Word for discernment rather than looking elsewhere for answers to your problems?

7. What role does prayer play in your everyday life? How can you discipline yourself to pray without ceasing?

Prayer

Lord, I am far more self-reliant than I should be. Far too often, I default into "fix it" mode rather than lean upon Your Word for wisdom and discernment. It seems easier to trust my instincts than stop what I am doing and pray for Your help. I find myself turning to the wrong people for advice instead of seeking counsel from wise, Biblical counselors. No wonder I am so lost at times! Help me lean upon You, first and foremost, before looking to those who would only tell me what I want to hear. Only You have the power to save my soul from self-destruction and redirect my path toward safety. Please teach me to follow Your commands rather than rely upon myself amid trials and tribulations. Amen.

CHAPTER 3

Help! I Am Enslaved

(I'm tired of my addiction to sin.)

O ne of the most common misconceptions about becoming a follower of Jesus Christ is that life will be easy once we make Him Lord and Savior. The assumption is that all our fleshly desires will miraculously fade away once the Holy Spirit enters our hearts. We will no longer crave things which once clouded our judgment and manipulated our actions. The problem is that even though the blood of Jesus cleanses us from all unrighteousness, we still have free will to choose which path we will take at any moment. The only difference is we are held accountable by God to maintain self-control and not revert to old, sinful patterns which formerly enslaved us.

"For freedom Christ has set us free; stand firm therefore, and do not submit again to a yoke of slavery."

— Galatians 5:1

Galatians 5:1 provides much-needed perspective because it reminds us that Christ set us free from the power of sin and death so we could live in freedom, not bondage. We can rest assured that sin has no power over us because Jesus' shed blood on the cross of Calvary paid for our sins. Therefore, our identity is found in Him alone, not the destructive pleasures of this world which once enslaved us. For the scarlet letter of our shameful past seeks to bind us to former sins and separate us from Christ, and we must avoid its deadly snare.

> *"And you were dead in the trespasses and sins in which you once walked, following the course of this world, following the prince of the power of the air, the spirit that is now at work in the sons of disobedience—among whom we all once lived in the passions of our flesh, carrying out the desires of the body and the mind, and were by nature children of wrath, like the rest of mankind."*
>
> — *Ephesians 2:1–3*

However, we are not lifeless robots that lack emotion, possess no free-will, and are programmable with 100% accuracy. What we desire with our physical senses appeals to our flesh. That means we have daily choices to make regarding whom or what we ultimately serve. As a result, we must build spiritual disciplines to guard our hearts and protect our minds from backsliding into destructive patterns which formerly enslaved us to false idols. Addiction to sinful behavior is no different than being enslaved to a particular idol because yielding to sin is the common thread in both scenarios.

Addiction is the epitome of destructive and abusive behavior. When we think about addiction, we typically attribute it to sexual immorality, substance abuse, gambling, or the pursuit of power, title, and financial gain. However, addiction encompasses a wide range of emotions, thoughts, and behaviors, both legal and illegal, in varying degrees. The challenge most of us have defining addictive behavior, whether we realize it or not, depends more on how we measure its severity than how it manifests itself in our daily lives.

> *"But now that you have been set free from sin and have become slaves of God, the fruit you get leads to sanctification and its end, eternal life. For the wages of sin is death, but the free gift of God is eternal life in Christ Jesus our Lord."*
>
> — *Romans 6:22–23*

If we are honest, our hierarchy of addictive behavior is nothing more than a justification scale weighed heavily against issues we rarely deal with, compared to sins which are daily struggles. For example, most people would classify consumption of narcotic drugs (cocaine, heroin, opioids, or crystal meth) at the top of their list of most destructive behaviors. However, where do various "legal" substances (alcohol, nicotine, marijuana, steroids, OTC's, or prescription painkillers) rank as well? Moreover, how do we feel about all forms of gambling, lust, pornography, binge-eating, compulsive shopping, videogaming, sports fantasy leagues, or social media which consume our time, energy, and resources?

Delving even deeper, how many of us struggle repeatedly with anxiety, gossiping, anger, jealousy, envy, impure thoughts, hard-heartedness, covetousness, laziness, complaining, negativity, or discontentment in God's provision (just to name a few)? Are we more likely to excuse addictive behaviors which are more socially acceptable and may not have immediate consequences, or do we consider all sins equal, regardless of severity, because they isolate us from God's grace and mercy? Sin separates us from God, yet we often maintain a mental list of acceptable sins and assume we are all good if we just avoid the bad ones. Why? What good does it serve to think more highly of ourselves than we ought and suffer the consequences of our naïve ignorance?

"Put to death therefore what is earthly in you: sexual immorality, impurity, passion, evil desire, and covetousness, which is idolatry."

— *Colossians 3:5*

The truth of the matter is we are all addicts, to one degree or another, because addiction is the result of continually yielding to habitual sin which we are guilty of regularly. However, we tend to compartmentalize addicts into their own category of deviance to justify sins we commit as less egregious in God's sight. That is not how sin works, though. Addiction impacts us all whether we realize it or not. Therefore, we must own our self-righteousness and repent of our judgment against others, for they are no better or worse than we are when we yield to fleshly desires daily and succumb to temptation.

One of the common mistakes we make regarding enslavement to addictive patterns is misdiagnosing sin as a disease rather than a conscious and volitional choice. Treating it as a disease merely puts an addict in a victimization mindset which further perpetuates the problem and offers no viable solution. However, to remedy the situation, we must shift our perspective, own our sins, and repent of our choices to replace the all-sufficiency of Christ with false idols. The longer we compartmentalize sin from a victim's mindset, the harder it will be to own our poor choices, repent of our transgressions, and break free from the chains of addiction which bind our hearts.

"For I know my transgressions, and my sin is ever before me. Against you, you only, have I sinned and done what is evil in your sight, so that you may be justified in your words and blameless in your judgment."

— *Psalm 51:3–4*

The enemy wants us to justify our sins and blame shift who is at fault because he knows that ownership begins the redemptive journey toward repentance. He also wants us to minimize our sins as not nearly as bad as they might seem. That is why Satan tempts us to run away from personal responsibility to appease our flesh. He wants us to deflect attention off what we need to change which is the selfishness of our hearts. He knows that if we are consumed with determining exactly who or what influenced our behavior, outside of ourselves, we will be distracted enough to remain shackled to the stronghold of addiction rather than take the necessary measures to change our behavior.

Without question, the enemy does not want us to own the consequences of our actions. Instead, he wants us to point the finger at outside influences to blame shift and justify our foolish decisions. That is why Paul encourages, **"Stand firm therefore, and do not submit again to a yoke of slavery" (Gal. 5:1),** because we are no longer slaves to sin but set free by the power of Jesus' blood. Granted, the skeletons of our past will always feel more familiar no matter how much time passes. Therefore, we must submit to the absolute truth and authority of God's Word as our source of strength to change direction and begin living for righteousness.

Scripture helps us distinguish between right and wrong and reminds us of the consequences of sin to hold us accountable. However, a man who holds onto an escape clause from taking personal responsibility is not living in freedom. His debased mind is merely planning to fail because he has misdiagnosed his addiction as outside of his influence and self-control. I know the mind game all too well. I once struggled with an addiction to pornography yet justified it as a necessary means to an end when my fleshly desires were not being met. I expected my wife to do whatever I wanted whenever I desired. If not, I felt that yielding to pornography was warranted.

Overcoming addiction (in any form) is made possible if we are willing to relinquish full control of our lives to God and His sovereignty, no matter the cost. That may seem easy to preach on the surface but making amends for sins committed against those we love is completely different. It takes an incredible amount of humility and courage to look someone in the eye and confess our iniquity, but it is a critical component of rehabilitation because we cannot move forward without reconciling our past. That is why godly grief and Biblical repentance go hand-in-hand. They force us to see our sins from God's holy perspective.

"The sacrifices of God are a broken spirit; a broken and contrite heart, O God, you will not despise."

— *Psalm 51:17*

True rehabilitation follows a pattern of Biblical repentance which cycles through (1) mourning our sins wholeheartedly, (2) owning the consequences of our actions, (3) confessing our sins to those we have hurt, (4) humbly asking for forgiveness, and (5) restoring our broken relationships by making permanent changes to reject sin and live for Christ. Each step is critically important to ensure we comprehend the gravity of our foolishness and what is required to bring genuine repentance full circle.

However, to live completely free from the shackles of our past, we must allow God to fill the seismic void our sins once held. Otherwise, we will relapse into old patterns and revert to sinful behaviors which promise peace and comfort but only enslave us further. Filling our lives with new spiritual disciplines and healthy relationships is critical to long-term survival. They each hold us accountable and protect us from further harm. However, if we fail to implement new disciplines, the enemy will merely enslave us again and hold us hostage to the demands of our carnal desires.

"When the unclean spirit has gone out of a person, it passes through waterless places seeking rest, and finding none it says, 'I will return to my house from which I came.' And when it comes, it finds the house swept and put in order. Then it goes and brings seven other spirits more evil than itself, and they enter and dwell there. And the last state of that person is worse than the first."

— Luke 11:24–26

Breaking free from addiction is a matter of faith in the absolute truth of God's Word. However, do we believe Jesus is truly the answer to all our problems? Oftentimes, Scripture can feel like nothing more than ink on a page when we are tired and weary. How then do we break free when temptation overwhelms our senses? Can we escape making poor decisions and avoid relapsing into former addictions? In many ways, it comes down to whether we trust God's ability to free us from addiction.

Those going through rehabilitation know that past addictions serve no present benefit, yet many revert to old patterns because they minimize sins and become desensitized to the consequences of their actions. That is why the only remedy to overcoming addiction is true worship of Christ. For when we find ourselves at fork-in-the-road decisions and trials of life have us longing to escape reality, the temptation to obey our fleshly cravings feels like the easiest solution. However, it only leads us into further problems because we are worshipping false idols instead of our sovereign Creator.

"But if we walk in the light, as he is in the light, we have fellowship with one another, and the blood of Jesus his Son cleanses us from all sin. If we say we have no sin, we deceive ourselves, and the truth is not in us. If we confess our sins, he is faithful and just to forgive us our sins and to cleanse

us from all unrighteousness."

— 1 John 1:7–9

It also does us no good to merely cut off the supply line to our addictions and expect complete victory. Rather, we must mortally wound our enemy with the light of Christ to ensure Satan never tempts us again to doubt the absolute truth of Scripture. Chances are we may still relapse into old, sinful patterns, but that does not mean the changes we have made are a waste. It simply indicates that we momentarily took our eyes off Christ and must repent of our sins to not fall victim to temptation again.

"For we all stumble in many ways. And if anyone does not stumble in what he says, he is a perfect man, able also to bridle his whole body."

— James 3:2

Building spiritual disciplines takes quality time, intentionality, consistency, determination, and patience. That does not mean we will never sin again. It simply means we are guarding against it. However, if we do fall, we must confess our sins, repent of our failures, and continue walking in the light of Christ. Satan wants us to believe we must return to the starting line when we relapse, but that is a lie. We simply need to recognize our sinful patterns and continue our sanctification journey from where we last fell.

Addiction from sin does not have to be a scarlet letter we bear publicly. We are not defined by our past or present, but by Jesus who died to set us free from sin's bondage. Therefore, rather than wallow in our guilt, shame, and regret, let us allow God to use our stories to bring glory to His name. Confessing sins publicly demands humility as we expose our vulnerability and risk being judged, but it is also the door to freedom from bondage.

"Faith in Jesus is not the heritage of the slaves of sin and Satan. It is the portion of those who are free men and women in Christ Jesus. If He has made you free, you are free indeed, and you can never be enslaved again."

— *Charles Spurgeon*
"The Blood of Christ's Covenant," November 12, 1863.

God does miraculous work when we step outside our comfort zone and relinquish our fear of man. Oftentimes, we can distract ourselves from revealing our personal struggles because we worry what people might think. Nevertheless, confessing our sins allows others to witness how God restores and redeems those held captive by temptation. It provides them hope which they desperately need to overcome fear and doubt regarding their ability to gain victory once and for all.

Why then would we ever cower from praising God and giving Him the glory He deserves for saving us? We all need to hear personal testimonies of deliverance from the bondage of sin to inspire change. The same holds true for others. If we have been healed, restored, rehabilitated, and redeemed by God's grace from the powers of hell, our stories are no longer our own. They belong to the Lord, and we are called to trust His sovereignty while He uses our testimonies to minister to those who likewise share our personal struggles.

Our past is filled with decisions we deeply regret, but God can use them for His glory if we lay down our selfish pride, humble ourselves, and walk by faith in His sovereign will for our lives. The more we talk about how God has redeemed us, the greater opportunity there will be for others to find victory, because our stories are not our own. They belong to God and we are merely His messengers of grace and mercy to a lost world devoid of hope and enslaved to sin and temptation.

Application

1. Which sins once enslaved you? Which still hold a grip on your heart to this day? Why?

2. Which triggers (such as pain, stress, loneliness, or boredom) cause you to yield to temptation?

3. How have you allowed your mind to compartmentalize sin as a disease rather than a conscious decision to disobey God?

4. Why is ownership and personal responsibility hypercritical to overcoming sinful addictions?

5. Which step in the Biblical repentance cycle are you struggling to reconcile in your heart and mind? How so?

6. What is your greatest takeaway from Luke 11:24-26? Why?

7. What changes can you make to remove sin at its root rather than allowing it to grow back over time?

Prayer

Lord, it takes an incredible amount of humility to waive the white flag of surrender and admit I have been enslaved to sin. My flesh wants me to minimize and justify my foolish decisions, but I cannot escape the fact that I own my sins and must reconcile my past before Your throne. I know that I not only need to eliminate temptations from my life but replace them with healthy, spiritual disciplines to protect my soul moving forward. Help me loathe my sins so I am inspired and empowered to change my wicked ways. I long to be free from the chains of bondage to false idols. Help me trust the Spirit's guidance and not assume I can defeat the enemy without You. Amen.

CHAPTER 4

Lord, Give Me Freedom
(Remind me of who I am in Christ.)

If you were asked to give your personal faith testimony of how God freed you from the power of sin and death, how would you respond? Would you politely decline or seriously consider the opportunity to share how Jesus radically changed your life? It is a big decision. However, truth be told, many of us hesitate to reveal our stories of heart change and transformation because we are afraid of what others might think if they knew which dark sins formerly enslaved us.

Truly, the greatest challenge with sharing one's testimony is that when we reveal the skeletons of our past, there is no going back. What once was hidden and private suddenly becomes public knowledge, and there is no way to determine whether others will look at us the same once they know how wretched and sinful we were and still may be. All we can do is trust that the Lord will give us strength to endure whatever comes our way after we share the intimate details of our past.

Spiritual warfare is intense for those who have never publicly shared their faith testimony, for the enemy knows which buttons to push to make us fear man's rejection, doubt God's provision, and worry about things we cannot control. How then should we respond? Will we remain silent and keep our personal testimonies general at best, or will we risk our personal comforts and allow the Lord to use our stories in supernatural ways to advance the Gospel of salvation for lost souls?

"Therefore, if anyone is in Christ, he is a new creation. The old has passed away; behold, the new has come."

— 2 Corinthians 5:17

The most critical thing we must remember sharing our faith testimony is it has nothing to do with us, for Christ rescued our hearts, redeemed our souls, and restored the joy of our salvation. Only through His shed blood are we cleansed and made whole. So, what causes us to hesitate from sharing our story of redemption if we are glorifying God and not ourselves? The greatest tactic Satan uses to stop us is presumed embarrassment. We think, "If others knew what God knows about me, they would never look at me the same way."

However, in believing such lies we deter advancing the Gospel because we are more focused on our personal reputation than the Lord's provision. Testimonies of faith and heart change have incredible power to influence others. They force us to shift our attention on what God has done in and through us, not what we have done through good works to earn His favor. Thus, when we share our testimonies, we are magnifying the power of Christ and how He has freed us from sin.

"But God, being rich in mercy, because of the great love with which he loved us, even when we were dead in our trespasses, made us alive together with Christ—by grace you have been saved."

— Ephesians 2:4–5

"But when the goodness and loving kindness of God our Savior appeared, he saved us, not because of works done by us in righteousness, but according to his own mercy, by the washing of regeneration and renewal of the Holy Spirit, whom he poured out on us richly through Jesus Christ our Savior."

— *Titus 3:4–6*

The enemy can often bait us into worrying about how our testimonies reflect who we are, past and present. However, that is not the reason God calls us to evangelize by means of sharing our personal stories of victory over sin and death. We share because our testimonies of forgiveness, grace, and mercy allow others to see themselves through our struggles, so that they too might break free from the chains of isolation and bondage which enslave their hearts to hopelessness and despair.

God's grace and mercy are magnified when we share how lost we once were and how incapable we are to save ourselves. Only by the blood of Jesus did God purchase, restore, and redeem us. He provided freedom from our sins and powerful testimonies to share. How then could we not give Him all the glory, honor, and praise He is due? The least we can do is abandon our worldly fears and trust His sovereign Word, which reminds us of who we are in Christ compared to our lost, former selves apart from Him.

The key to giving a God-honoring testimony is discerning which details we should share to give context and understanding concerning our redemption in Christ. Nevertheless, success is far more contingent upon the reasons why we share than the specific details themselves. That is why fervent prayer and wise counsel are so important in preparing our testimonies to ensure our focus is always on Jesus. Prayer keeps our hearts and minds in tune with the Spirit's conviction as we navigate which details are pertinent vs. distracting to the story at large and essentially inconsequential.

In some cases, personal testimonies are shared. Therefore, it is critical we are sensitive to the hearts of those who have been impacted by our sins and respect their privacy. For example, if a man's testimony involves confession of sins such as adultery, it would be wise for him to talk with his wife beforehand and get her blessing before divulging details of their mutual past. That does not mean he should not share how God rescued him from sin, redeemed his heart, and restored their marriage. Rather, it means he must be sensitive to his wife's feelings to ensure she feels safe, edified, and protected from spiritual warfare which will impact her heart and mind when he reveals his testimony.

"Likewise, husbands, live with your wives in an understanding way, showing honor to the woman as the weaker vessel, since they are heirs with you of the grace of life, so that your prayers may not be hindered."

— *1 Peter 3:7*

If we are honest with ourselves, the greater struggle we face is reconciling the guilt, shame, and regret we bear because of sins. God does not want us to bear them alone. Instead, He wants us to release those burdens back to Him as a sacrificial offering of genuine repentance and lay them at the foot of the cross. When we do, we will discover lasting freedom which our hearts desperately crave because we are no longer subjecting our minds to the memories of former sins.

Far too often, we hold onto our past like a scarlet letter and identify who we are now by who we once were. The longer we cling to the past, the greater opportunity Satan is provided to keep us enslaved to former sins which cause us to be weary and restless. Therefore, we have a critical choice to make. We can either accept eternal salvation made possible by the atoning blood of Jesus or hold onto past memories and allow them to torment our hearts and minds forever. It all depends on whether we allow guilt, shame, and regret to define our identity.

Becoming a new creation does not mean we forget past sins because those memories, albeit painful to remember, play a vital role in keeping us humble. We must never take for granted the immeasurable sacrifice Jesus made on our behalf. Keep in mind, guilt, shame, and regret can serve two different purposes. They can be used by Satan to keep us in bondage to the destruction we caused or redeemed by God as a catalyst for heart change. One draws us closer to the cross of Calvary in genuine repentance. The other keeps us enslaved to the enemy.

Granted, memories will remain engrained within to give us a reverent posture before God in steadfast obedience to His holy Word. They are the residual blessings of salvation and new life in Christ, not something we should avoid or be ashamed of because they keep us accountable. Our inability to forget portions of the past is part of God's master plan, for it provides accountability while ensuring we are dependent upon God's grace and mercy for survival.

"For I am not ashamed of the gospel, for it is the power of God for salvation to everyone who believes, to the Jew first and also to the Greek. For in it the righteousness of God is revealed from faith for faith, as it is written, 'The righteous shall live by faith.'"

— Romans 1:16–17

Where the rubber meets the road for many souls attempting to overcome their fear of giving a personal testimony hinges upon their ability to shift perspective from darkness to light and discover the silver-lining of God's grace woven throughout their story. Without question, we are given free will by God to choose which path we will take in life. However, God will not force our hand to act in a certain way. Rather, He waits patiently with open arms to welcome us home, so long as we turn from our wicked ways and accept His immeasurable gift of salvation.

"For all have sinned and fall short of the glory of God, and are justified by his grace as a gift, through the redemption that is in Christ Jesus."

— *Romans 3:23–24*

When we reconcile our hearts to God, we are set free from the chains of sin which formerly enslaved us. However, our past and present are forever intertwined because our former depravity and sinful bents are the catalysts God uses to draw us home. In other words, what the enemy intends for evil, God utilizes for our benefit (Gen. 50:20). He will not abandon nor forsake us despite our poor choices but draw us unto Himself through genuine repentance. That is the miraculous power of God at work, turning ashes to beauty and using what the enemy meant for evil to sanctify and develop our personal character.

Memories also have a way of holding us captive to the past and stifling our growth, because the enemy is determined to remind us at every turn how sinful and wretched we used to be. Satan never wants us to forget the collateral damage and pain we caused because his intent is to bait us into questioning the true authenticity of heart change and doubt whether our identity in Christ is real. As a result, he aims to pin us down with guilt, shame, and regret because he knows they are powerful weapons strategically designed to remind us of our failures and the wake of destruction we caused.

"But I am afraid that as the serpent deceived Eve by his cunning, your thoughts will be led astray from a sincere and pure devotion to Christ."

— 2 Corinthians 11:3

I have long held that the thorn in the flesh which tormented Paul throughout his ministry was not physical at all, but spiritual. Keep in mind, he gave his approval for the stoning of Stephen and vehemently persecuted the church by having followers of Christ beaten, imprisoned, and killed. Paul was determined to eradicate Christians at all costs. However, Jesus stopped him dead in his tracks on the Damascus road and converted him of all people to be a missionary. God chose Paul to preach the Gospel of salvation to the Gentiles rather than live as an obsessed, religious oppressor of Christianity.

Yet no matter how passionately Paul preached and endured persecution on behalf of Jesus, he could not escape the memories of his past. Every city he visited, his reputation preceded him, which meant the atrocities of his former self and acts of violence against Christ-followers were always at the forefront of his mind. Nevertheless, rather than be crippled by his shameful past, Paul used it as a backdrop for his faith testimony, allowing God to be glorified through his weakness. Paul understood that his story was no longer his own but a catalyst to glorify the Lord. He determined his mind to suffer mightily if it meant Christ was glorified, and God honored his sacrifice.

"For I am the least of the apostles, unworthy to be called an apostle, because I persecuted the church of God. But by the grace of God I am what I am, and his grace toward me was not in vain."

— 1 Corinthians 15:9–10

Paul dealt with thorns of guilt, shame, and regret on a regular basis, yet it did not deter him from his calling. Instead, his former reputation inspired him to remain humbly dependent on Jesus as his sole source of strength amid violent attacks, imprisonment, floggings, and inevitably, death. That is why Paul praised God for his thorns of persecution and accepted the spiritual warfare they inevitably produced, because Jesus was glorified in and through them. In other words, while He was being tortured for his faith in Christ, God was working behind the scenes to provide greater opportunities to share the Gospel with those in prison and in authority positions as well.

> *"So to keep me from becoming conceited because of the surpassing greatness of the revelations, a thorn was given me in the flesh, a messenger of Satan to harass me, to keep me from becoming conceited. Three times I pleaded with the Lord about this, that it should leave me. But he said to me, 'My grace is sufficient for you, for my power is made perfect in weakness.' Therefore I will boast all the more gladly of my weaknesses, so that the power of Christ may rest upon me. For the sake of Christ, then, I am content with weaknesses, insults, hardships, persecutions, and calamities. For when I am weak, then I am strong."*
>
> *— 2 Corinthians 12:7–10*

The beauty of Paul's ministry was that he was unafraid to talk about his past. He knew God would use his personal testimony to inspire others to turn from their wicked ways. He certainly could have chosen to never speak again of his past. Instead, he embraced it with humility because he understood that his story was no longer his own. God had rescued, redeemed, and restored Paul for eternity. Therefore, every time he gave his personal testimony, he was sharing God's story of redemption in Christ. He offered his life as a sacrificial offering for others to identify with and learn from, and God mightily blessed his efforts.

> *"I thank him who has given me strength, Christ Jesus our Lord, because*

he judged me faithful, appointing me to his service, though formerly I was a blasphemer, persecutor, and insolent opponent. But I received mercy because I had acted ignorantly in unbelief, and the grace of our Lord overflowed for me with the faith and love that are in Christ Jesus. The saying is trustworthy and deserving of full acceptance, that Christ Jesus came into the world to save sinners, of whom I am the foremost. But I received mercy for this reason, that in me, as the foremost, Jesus Christ might display his perfect patience as an example to those who were to believe in him for eternal life.”

— 1 Timothy 1:12–16

Giving a personal testimony is not easy but necessary for advancing the Gospel of salvation. People need to see how Jesus can come alive and transform the heart of a man. Our culture is desperately searching for hope in a lost world, but breaking free from past sins is difficult. The enemy wants to keep us enslaved to fear, doubt, and worry to silence our message of hope. Thus, we must remember that those who are struggling to break free from various sin addictions need a victorious example to follow. God can use what the enemy meant for evil and turn it for good, but we must trust Him and never doubt. Our testimonies can be instruments of righteousness God uses to save the lost, but we must share them boldly and not be afraid. Christ has freed us from sin and death by His shed blood. Whom then shall we fear other than the Lord almighty (Psa. 27:1)?

“But in your hearts honor Christ the Lord as holy, always being prepared to make a defense to anyone who asks you for a reason for the hope that is in you; yet do it with gentleness and respect.”

— 1 Peter 3:15

Application

1. Why is it so important to reflect upon and share your personal faith testimony?

2. Which details of your testimony should you seek counsel and permission before sharing publicly?

3. How has God used guilt, shame, and regret for your benefit? How has the enemy intended them for evil instead?

4. What role do memories play in keeping you humble and solely dependent upon Christ for strength and salvation?

5. Which mental, emotional, or spiritual thorns of the flesh do you struggle with most? How so?

6. How have you been able to shift your perspective and thank God for your weaknesses?

7. How has God created beauty from the ashes of your sins?

Prayer

Lord, sometimes I wander aimlessly through life still shackled to the memories of my past. I tend to hide from the guilt, shame, and regret of my former self and not use my testimony of faith as a platform to share Your Gospel. Help me to never forget who I once was so I remain solely dependent on You. Thank You for allowing me to see my sins clearly and the wake of destruction I caused. I never want to be enslaved again to my flesh. You have blessed me beyond measure and I want to share what You have done in and through me for Your glory. My freedom is in You alone, Lord, and I am eternally grateful for Your priceless gift of salvation. Amen.

CHAPTER 5

Help! I Am Anxious
(I'm tired of worrying about tomorrow.)

I f we desire to find rest for our weary souls, we must confront our anxious feelings, which Satan uses to torment our minds, and put a plan of action in place to earn victory. No matter how hard we try, we cannot discover peace and contentment if we are unwilling to trust the Lord and reject the wisdom of our own understanding. Our primary goal should always be to guard our minds from allowing anxiety to wage war against our psyche, and that inevitably begins with asking ourselves why we are anxious in the first place.

"Why are you cast down, O my soul, and why are you in turmoil within me? Hope in God; for I shall again praise him, my salvation."

— Psalm 42:5

Anxiety is often a dysfunctional security blanket we use to protect us from the vast and indescribable unknown. Anxiety will never solve our questions or concerns either. Nevertheless, fear, doubt, and worry are familiar and comfortable when we crave something tangible to hold onto amid the storms of life. In many ways, anxiety is like an unhealthy relationship which seems impossible to leave. No matter how hard we try or how often we rationalize letting go, we revert to the same abusive relationship we long to escape from because we cannot fully reconcile what lies ahead.

However, there is hope in Christ! For in Philippians 4:4-7, Paul prescribes joy and thankfulness as the critical antidote to cure our minds from the stronghold of anxiety and free us from bondage. In turn, it enables us to effectively commune with God in prayer because peace of heart, mind, and soul are found when we relinquish anxiety and allow the Holy Spirit to wash our minds with the water of God's Word. Moreover, prayer enables us to release our feelings as we purge our minds of anxious thoughts in preparation for what God has in store to teach us.

"Rejoice in the Lord always; again I will say, rejoice. Let your reasonableness be known to everyone. The Lord is at hand; do not be anxious about anything, but in everything by prayer and supplication with thanksgiving let your requests be made known to God. And the peace of God, which surpasses all understanding, will guard your hearts and your minds in Christ Jesus."

— Philippians 4:4–7

Supernaturally, joy overrides the circuitry of our brain and refocuses our attention on what God has graciously provided rather than what we selfishly lack. It prepares our hearts and cleanses our minds so we can cast our cares upon the Lord. In the end, it is peace of mind which we desperately need more than ever when the walls are closing in. For if we fail to guard our minds from the dangers of doubt and worry, we will never receive God's perfect peace which surpasses all understanding and allows us to live worry free.

If we are called to rejoice in the Lord as Paul affirms, where does reasonableness fit into the equation? Most Bible translations use gentleness in place of reasonableness which provides context to this passage. Moreover, if we filter Philippians 4:4 through what we read in James 1:2, rejoicing or counting it joy when we face trials of various kinds will perplex those around us. They do not share our doctrine of faith nor comprehend our radical behavior. Therefore, we should not be surprised if others struggle understanding our thankfulness amid trials when it appears on the surface that there is nothing to be thankful about. That is why the Gospel is so countercultural.

"Count it all joy, my brothers, when you meet trials of various kinds."

— James 1:2

Sometimes, life punches us right in the face. Whether it be our own sin issues, health-related challenges, victimization, or something completely different, trials can rock our world and leave us paralyzed with apprehension. However, God still has a plan and purpose for our trials even when we cannot find a silver-lining in the moment. That does not mean we ignore our feelings which can tempt us to be anxious. Rather, we focus on God's grace and mercy which are woven throughout our trials, for they give meaning and purpose to the lessons God teaches us amid pain, difficulty, and hardship.

"The natural person does not accept the things of the Spirit of God, for they are folly to him, and he is not able to understand them because they are spiritually discerned."

— 1 Corinthians 2:14

I have found that when I am struggling with anxiety and my stress level is through the roof, the last thing I want to do is count my trials as joy and smile in the face of overwhelming despair and trepidation. In the moment, I do not want to hear that God has a divine plan and purpose for my life which will all work out in the end. When nothing appears to be going right, I feel paralyzed by the future because it is unknown. It is a frightening position to find oneself but also a prime opportunity for God to show up in a supernatural way and change our perspective regarding His providence and provision. In other words, God creates a spiritual marker opportunity.

Early in our marriage, we struggled to make ends meet. Due to employment relocation, we were financially stretched beyond our means in a geographical area where the cost of living was substantially higher than we expected. Expenses exceeded our monthly income despite our best efforts to cut costs and pinch pennies. Unfortunately, we found ourselves in the red due to hospital bills following the birth of our first daughter. We did not know what to do being new parents except pray that God would protect us. In that moment, anxiety overwhelmed our minds until we laid our stress and worry at the foot of the cross and allowed God to intervene supernaturally.

What we experienced was an outpouring of love from our extended families who knew we were trying our best but could not reconcile the cost of our hospital bills. Unbeknownst to us, resources were pooled together and we were handed a check to cover down on our financial shortage. Finally, we could rest easy. Moreover, the hospital partially refunded us for overcharges. In hindsight, all we needed was to trust the Lord, knowing that our season of trial was meant to strengthen our faith, not deter it. It did not feel joyous in the moment, but God taught us a valuable lesson about releasing our burdens to Him and not stressing over details to the point of hopelessness and despair.

"Humble yourselves, therefore, under the mighty hand of God so that at the proper time he may exalt you, casting all your anxieties on him, because he cares for you."

— *1 Peter 5:6–7*

Counting trials as joy is as illogical as it gets. It makes no sense to praise God when we are overwhelmed with anxiety to the point of losing self-control entirely. However, that is how Christ-followers are expected to act when life comes crashing down. Jesus willingly endured pain and hardship on our behalf to provide an eternal way of escape from sin and death. Therefore, we are expected to emulate His example by sharing our testimony that trials can be blessings rather than curses if we look for the silver-lining of God's grace and mercy.

Keep in mind, we should treat unbelievers with compassion when they fail to believe or understand God's Word. Because they do not share the same Biblical standard of truth, we must extend grace as they struggle to understand how radical a response joy truly is in the face of anxiety. It is critical we do not gloss over the importance of gentleness with those who question how joy and thankfulness could be viable solutions for someone plagued by stress and anxiety. They do not hold the same level of understanding. Thus, they cannot begin to understand why trials could be blessings rather than curses.

"But I say to you who hear, Love your enemies, do good to those who hate you, bless those who curse you, pray for those who abuse you. To one who strikes you on the cheek, offer the other also, and from one who takes away your cloak do not withhold your tunic either."

— *Luke 6:27–29*

When we read Philippians 4:4-7, we tend to jump to the punchline, **"Do not be anxious about anything,"** without taking time to consider why we should not be anxious, **"for the Lord is at hand."** Scripture is full of reminders which point to God's faithfulness amid the storms of life, strengthening those who call upon His name and delivering those who are persecuted for righteousness' sake. However, it is critical we comprehend the gravity of God's presence during our trials to avoid assuming we are lost and all alone.

"My flesh and my heart may fail, but God is the strength of my heart and my portion forever."

— Psalm 73:26

Despite what the enemy might tempt us to believe, God is not surprised by our anxiety. He knows we lack knowledge, wisdom, and understanding to discern how we should respond to trials in the moment. That is why He bestows grace when we are anxious and fail to recognize the true intimacy of His presence. He also demonstrates great patience when we continually question His sovereign authority. We tend to forget that He knows us better than we know ourselves, which is why we can rest confidently that He knows what we need and will provide for us in His way and timing.

"A man of many companions may come to ruin, but there is a friend who sticks closer than a brother."

— Proverbs 18:24

Prayer is also critical to overcoming anxiety. It is the bridge which connects our hearts to God and allows us to release our anxious thoughts to Him so we are no longer held captive by fear and worry but free to worship Him. Prayer keeps the line of communication open with God which we desperately need to overcome anxiety. However, prayer does not necessarily solve our problems. It merely shifts the attention off our trials and refocuses them on the only one who can do anything about them: Jesus Christ.

Prayer also enables us to break free from the chains of isolation by reestablishing our heart-connection to God, aligning our personal will with His, and replacing our anxious thoughts with thankfulness. It is a direct line of communication whereby we can release all our pent-up emotions and lay them at the foot of the cross. Keep in mind, we are not enslaved to a rollercoaster of emotions. We are more than conquerors through Christ who strengthens us. That is why prayer is our greatest method of expressing our hearts to the Father because He is always ready and waiting to hear what we have to say.

When it comes to anxiety, peace is our pearl of great price, for nothing satisfies our hearts and minds more than relinquishing fear, doubt, and worry for the last time. However, peace of mind is only achievable when we relinquish control and trust God with our unforeseen future, no matter the outcome. That may seem easy to implement, but reality is completely different when the storms of life rage within our minds. It begs the question, have we ever considered that anxiety exposes our lack of faith and trust in God's sovereignty? More importantly, do we recognize our depravity of faith in the Lord's strength and provision, or are we too naïve to think He cannot overcome our anxiety?

"If any of you lacks wisdom, let him ask God, who gives generously to all without reproach, and it will be given him. But let him ask in faith, with no doubting, for the one who doubts is like a wave of the sea that is driven

and tossed by the wind. For that person must not suppose that he will receive anything from the Lord; he is a double-minded man, unstable in all his ways."

— James 1:5–8

Oftentimes, we function as if the weight of our anxiety is so great that not even God Himself can bear it. We tighten our grip and muscle our way through trials only to burn out from mental fatigue, physical exhaustion, and emotional collapse. However, God is patient despite our lack of faith and continues to bless us even though we continually doubt Him. He knows our trust in Him is far more conditional than unconditional. Nevertheless, He blesses us even though we do not deserve it. For He loves us not because of who we are, but because of who He is as perfector of our souls.

It is sobering to realize that anxiety reveals our spiritual maturity (or lack thereof), but it is something we must reconcile in our minds and own in our hearts. No Christian desires to be considered spiritually shallow in faith. However, the more we succumb to fear, doubt, and worry, the more we prove how little we trust God unconditionally and wholeheartedly. That might be a hard pill to swallow, but trials expose who we are on the inside and prove whom we ultimately trust during seasons of anxiety.

That is why trusting the Lord is the key to unlocking peace that surpasses all human understanding. It removes us from the battlefield of spiritual warfare and substitutes Jesus in our place to fight our battles. Why then would we ever allow worry to hold more power and control over our minds than God? Jesus died to set us free, not leave us chained in bondage to sin forevermore. What power then does anxiety possess? Did Christ not defeat our fear, doubt, and worry when He gave his life on the cross for our sins and resurrected three days later?

Anxiety is a sensitive issue because it is personal and convicting. However, Scripture is clear that stress and worry should have no place in the hearts and minds of Christ-followers. Rather, our faith, hope, and trust in the Lord must overpower our propensity to obsess about things we have no power to control. Without Christ, we are unable to save ourselves from the enemy's stronghold, so why do we even attempt? Truly, we are far better served relinquishing control of our emotions to Jesus and surrendering them at the foot of the cross.

We hold no power in and of ourselves to overcome the forces of darkness in our lives. Only God is all-powerful and capable of defeating sin and death. Thus, we are wise to relinquish control to Him because He alone can save us. Truly, we often obsess over hypothetical scenarios which may never come to fruition. Would we not be better served trusting the Lord, obeying His Word, and allowing His peace to become our strength instead of fear, doubt, and worry? If the Lord is with us, who can be against us? Satan holds no power over us if we are in Christ.

"Therefore do not be anxious about tomorrow, for tomorrow will be anxious for itself. Sufficient for the day is its own trouble."

— Matthew 6:34

None of us are guaranteed tomorrow, so why should we live deathly afraid of the future? Truly, we are better off trusting the Lord and focusing our attention on what we can manage, compared to future events which overwhelm our minds, consume our attention, and inevitably may never come to pass. None of us can predict the future either. Therefore, worrying about what trials tomorrow may bring is pointless. God alone is sovereign over all creation, so we have nothing to fear because He is in control and always has our best interest in mind.

Application

1. Why is there dysfunctional comfort yielding to anxiety rather than guarding against it? What benefit does it serve?

2. How can you incorporate more joy and gratitude to God in your daily routine?

3. Do you believe God allows trials to happen or causes them? Why? What difference does it make?

4. What is your blunt and honest opinion regarding James 1:2? How is your ability to share the Gospel impacted by it?

5. Is prayer typically your first response or last resort to overcoming anxiety? Why?

6. How can anxiety begin to draw you closer to God rather than farther away from Him?

7. Why is anxiety a far greater issue of the heart than the mind?

Prayer

Lord, there is so much in this world to be anxious about and I often get worried about tomorrow that I forget to live for today. Help me count my blessings, knowing You have the universe in the palm of Your hands and will work all things for my good. Anxiety is a far greater issue of faith than I care to admit, and I have fallen woefully short of trusting You with every aspect of my life. Please forgive me for acting as if my problems are too big for You. Give me patience to yield to Your sovereign timing when the storms of life linger much longer than I desire. I know that trials are meant to draw me closer to You, so help me die to anxiety and walk in the light of Your truth forevermore. Amen.

CHAPTER 6

Lord, Give Me Assurance
(Help me trust Your sovereignty.)

In today's world, it is often difficult to not be disappointed by someone or something. We live in a broken and fallen world and human beings are far from perfect. Truth be told, our loved ones often inflict the most damage to our psyche, whether intentional or not, and plunge us into a state of despair. However, at some point, our hopes, dreams, assumptions, and expectations are bound to come crashing down when life takes an unexpected turn or does not turn out how we think it should. Therefore, it is critical we level set our minds on truth which is absolute and not relative to guard our hearts from questioning the Lord and His omniscient sovereignty.

"Though the fig tree should not blossom, nor fruit be on the vines, the produce of the olive fail, and the fields yield no food, the flock be cut off from the fold and there be no herd in the stalls, yet I will rejoice in the LORD; I will take joy in the God of my salvation. GOD, the Lord, is my strength; he makes my feet like the deer's; he makes me tread on my high places."

— *Habakkuk 3:17–19*

Habakkuk 3:17-19 is such a breath of fresh air because it does not paint a rosy picture of life in Christ. It acknowledges personal difficulty and disappointment in circumstances we face yet lifts our eyes from the valley of despair and points our attention on a far greater mountaintop. More importantly, it affirms our faith and trust in Christ because He is the only one who can turn ashes to beauty and satisfy our weary souls amid seasons of fear, doubt, worry, and anxiety.

> *"The Spirit of the Lord GOD is upon me, because the LORD has anointed me to bring good news to the poor; he has sent me to bind up the brokenhearted, to proclaim liberty to the captives, and the opening of the prison to those who are bound; to proclaim the year of the LORD's favor, and the day of vengeance of our God; to comfort all who mourn; to grant to those who mourn in Zion—to give them a beautiful headdress instead of ashes, the oil of gladness instead of mourning, the garment of praise instead of a faint spirit; that they may be called oaks of righteousness, the planting of the LORD, that he may be glorified."*
>
> — *Isaiah 61:1–3*

As followers of Jesus Christ, we are not expected to wear a mask publicly or function as if everything is okay when clearly it is not. That type of behavior only perpetuates hypocrisy and a lack of authenticity which benefits no one. Instead, we are called to be transparent and real with others, sharing our struggles and exposing our vulnerability so that our testimony of God's grace has legitimacy when we speak of how faithful He has been despite our trials and disappointments.

It begs the question, what is a mountaintop summit without a valley below to give it context? The reason we can stand confident upon a cliff or peak is due to the deep valley below which provides a frame of reference regarding how far we have climbed.

Without the valley, there is no wonder, awe, and majesty of the horizon because they are dependent upon each other. Therefore, to appreciate the beauty of the horizon from the summit's ledge, we must praise God for the deep valleys or trials which give it proper context and perspective.

"Count it all joy, my brothers, when you meet trials of various kinds, for you know that the testing of your faith produces steadfastness. And let steadfastness have its full effect, that you may be perfect and complete, lacking in nothing."

— James 1:2–4

What James 1:2–4 teaches is as illogical and uncommon as any absolute truth in the Bible. How can we praise God when He allows pain and hardship to turn our lives upside down? Would anger and frustration not be a more appropriate response? Keep in mind, celebrating trials only makes the summit view that much sweeter. When we see how far God has brought us, we have a greater appreciation for the time-consuming and painstaking journey it took to get there. Our perspective changes because we can see God's hand at work in our struggles.

Oftentimes, we bristle at the mere thought of trials. We do not want to struggle in life or endure pain and hardship if we can help it, so we will do anything possible to avoid it altogether. However, life just does not work that way. We are bound to encounter trials which test our faith and expose what we are made of spiritually. Like a piece of fruit, what is inside us will come pouring out the minute hardship begins to squeeze our minds and constrict our faith. That is why trials are so useful for our sanctification. They help us gauge our spiritual maturity. For when life comes crashing down, our lack of faith will become blatantly obvious the minute we run away from God rather than seek His will.

As previously mentioned, when Amber and I were suddenly in a monetary crisis, there was no time available to get a second job or work out a different plan to earn income and cover down on our bills. My wife just had our first child, all our liabilities came due simultaneously, and we were overwhelmed with how we would pay for everything. Stress increased exponentially. We had never faced financial hardship before, but the fear of what to do next paralyzed us.

I would like to say what poured out when trials came knocking at our door was unwavering faith that the Lord would provide. However, as provider and protector of my family, I was fearful and anxious. How would I get us out of this mess? How would I shoulder the burden for my wife and daughter? It was up to me to figure it out, or so I thought in the moment, but God gently reminded me that it was not my burden to carry alone. In fact, He already had it completely worked out. I simply had to trust Him and not lose faith over minor details.

"In this you rejoice, though now for a little while, if necessary, you have been grieved by various trials, so that the tested genuineness of your faith—more precious than gold that perishes though it is tested by fire—may be found to result in praise and glory and honor at the revelation of Jesus Christ."

— 1 Peter 1:6–7

Whether we like it or not, personal character is refined during seasons of trials. Challenging circumstances expose our insecurities and the depth of our faith, forcing us to reconcile our fears. That is the essence of sanctification. Therefore, we should be less concerned with finding an escape route from our pain and sorrow and appreciate the unique perspective trials provide which draw us closer to the Lord in fasting and prayer.

No matter how hard we try, storms of life are impossible to avoid, even though we think we can outrun the dark clouds which continue to roll in. Yet when it rains, it pours, and far too many of us are soaked to the bone with countless setbacks which make us doubt whether God really cares or even hears our cries. Our minds have been drenched with anxiety for so long that we have forgotten how it feels to see ourselves in proper light. We have allowed fear, doubt, and worry to enslave us to hopelessness and despair.

It is difficult to remain steadfast in faith, hope, and trust in God when no relief comes from our anguish, or when trials continue to plague us with no end in sight. At times, silence from the Lord can cause us to turn our backs on His Word, doubt the power of prayer, or reject the body of Christ altogether when we are drowning in pain, sorrow, fatigue, and depression. However, it is in those moments when the depth and breadth of our faith is counted and measured. We discover whom we ultimately trust when push comes to shove.

"Behold, the LORD's hand is not shortened, that it cannot save, or his ear dull, that it cannot hear."

— Isaiah 59:1

The greatest position to be in during trials is the eye of the storm. Truly, there is silence there which allows the heart, mind, and soul to hear the Lord speaking—that is until wind and rain begin to rage again. The key for us in recalibrating our attention on the Spirit is distinguishing the storms which surround us from those which rage within and seek to undermine our trust in God's sovereignty. That is a critical distinction we must remember, for we often focus our attention on what is outside of our control than what is within our sphere of influence.

"Let your eyes look directly forward, and your gaze be straight before you. Ponder the path of your feet; then all your ways will be sure. Do not swerve to the right or to the left; turn your foot away from evil."

— *Proverbs 4:25–27*

Storms which surround us are the circumstantial details of the trials themselves (medical conditions, natural disasters, or financial difficulties). Those details are often out of our control which means we must accept them for what they are. Conversely, storms within us are completely different (misunderstanding, fear, or anger). They are emotionally driven and actually within our ability to exude self-control. The question is whether we want to reconcile our internal storms or remain consumed by the storms outside of our influence.

Habakkuk 3:17-19 gives multiple scenarios to help us identify the seasons of life we experience which inevitably test our faith and trust in the Lord. It is a powerful glimpse into the heart and mind of a godly man who struggled to reconcile trials which could have easily derailed his faith. Even though Habakkuk was a prophet of God, he struggled to find evidence of blessings, yet that did not deter him from praising the Lord and reminding himself that God was sovereign, even in hardship.

He acknowledged the blessings of God that were missing and lamented the expected, bountiful harvest which did not come to fruition. Yet even amid challenges, he chose to circumvent logic and focus on joy rather than sorrow and discontentment. He chose not to complain about the trials he faced which could have stolen his joy and fueled distrust in God's sovereignty. Rather, he praised the Lord for his hardships because he knew God's glory would inevitably be revealed through them, and he did not want to get in the way of God moving in his midst.

"Why are you cast down, O my soul, and why are you in turmoil within me? Hope in God; for I shall again praise him, my salvation, and my God."

— Psalm 43:5

What a declaration of faith, hope, and trust in the sovereignty of God! By choosing praise and thanksgiving despite difficult circumstances, Habakkuk's example is a testament of mind over matter by not allowing the enemy to plant seeds of doubt which tempt us to question God's provision. We are not slaves to our flesh if we are born-again in Christ but empowered to overcome our natural inclinations. We can choose how we will respond regardless of the outcome. Therefore, we need not fear the terror of the night because joy comes in the morning to those who trust in the Lord for salvation.

Surely, there will come a time when we will fail to see the fruits of our labor and doubt whether our faith journey efforts are worth it. Doubt and hopelessness will likely creep into our minds and tempt us to abandon faith in Christ altogether. Yet in those moments when temptation clouds our judgment, our faith has ample opportunity to grow exponentially. Thus, we are called to trust God's plan when we cannot see what is on the other side of the horizon and yield to His sovereign will.

We are not ill-equipped to manage what lies ahead, no matter the challenges we face. Just as Habakkuk asserts, our peace in the eye of the storm is knowing our salvation belongs to the Lord and He will not abandon His children. Rather, He will make our feet like that of a deer so we can tread among high places and reach the mountaintop where understanding and perspective are found. That does not mean God's peace will be easy to find. The difficult journey will likely test our faith, but we are comforted knowing the Lord hears our cries for help and protects our souls. He is forever faithful and will never forsake those who are within His care, no matter how many times we doubt His provision.

Confidence in the Lord is not a hopeless crutch we hold onto to brainwash our minds into thinking everything is fine when clearly it is not. True confidence is knowing that the Lord is still in control when storms rage, because He always has our best interest at heart despite our circumstances. We are not slaves to our flesh but born-again in the Spirit by grace through faith in Christ. Therefore, the same power which raised Jesus from the dead dwells in every man, woman, and child who professes Him as Lord and Savior. God's Spirit dwells inside of us if we confess the name of Jesus for eternal salvation, and He will guide our steps if we walk by faith in His holy Word.

Whether we realize it, we are not ill-equipped to manage our trials, nor must we succumb to fear, doubt, and worry which seem justified in the moment. Rather, God's Spirit empowers us to destroy every stronghold which tempts us to rely on ourselves when storms attempt to sink our faith. The key is washing our minds with the water of God's Word because it counteracts the lies which the enemy uses to rattle our faith and bait us into giving up. For we are more than conquerors through Christ, so there should be nothing to fear knowing Jesus conquered the grave on our behalf.

"Who shall separate us from the love of Christ? Shall tribulation, or distress, or persecution, or famine, or nakedness, or danger, or sword?"

— Romans 8:35

"No, in all these things we are more than conquerors through him who loved us. For I am sure that neither death nor life, nor angels nor rulers, nor things present nor things to come, nor powers, nor height nor depth,

nor anything else in all creation, will be able to separate us from the love of God in Christ Jesus our Lord."

— *Romans 8:37–39*

That does not mean we will never struggle understanding why we face trials and tribulations. Heaven knows we will! However, we should also have peace of mind despite our hardships because the Lord always has a specific purpose in mind for the struggles we face. It may not seem like it in the moment, but we know that seasons of life come and go. They bring death and rebirth to teach us more than we could ever ask for or imagine. We simply need to live by faith and not by sight, trusting that the Lord will reveal what we need to know, when the time comes, according to His sovereign will.

The real question is whether we will trust Him when our minds default into self-protection mode. There is nothing more difficult than learning to walk by faith in Christ when life batters and bruises us along the way. The enemy will whisper countless lies into our ears and bait us into giving up on the Lord, but we cannot yield to temptation. For He who began a magnificent work in us will not bring it to completion until the day we stand before the throne of grace and give account for our lives. On that day, our faith will be exposed for its merit. Therefore, we are wise to unconditionally trust the Lord if we expect to receive eternal assurance on judgment day.

"For my thoughts are not your thoughts, neither are your ways my ways, declares the LORD. For as the heavens are higher than the earth, so are my ways higher than your ways and my thoughts than your thoughts."

— *Isaiah 55:8–9*

Application

1. If you could ask God for one piece of complete assurance, what would it be? Why?

2. Why is it so dangerous to assume that nothing bad will ever happen when you place eternal faith in Jesus Christ?

3. How can you emulate Habakkuk's perspective and rejoice in the Lord when life does not turn out the way you assume?

4. Why is the eye of the storm the calmest place to be? What are the spiritual implications of abiding in Christ when storms rage in your life?

5. What can you praise God for considering the trials you are presently facing?

6. How has God assured that He is always with you despite the seasons of pain, suffering, and hardship you have endured or are currently facing?

Prayer

Lord, I know that trials are simply a part of life. No matter how hard I try, I cannot escape them. I admit it is difficult in the moment to find the silver-lining of Your grace and mercy, but I know it exists because You always pull me out of the ashes when I am on the verge of hopelessness. Why I continue to doubt Your sovereignty is a mystery. You have given me complete assurance through Christ that I am eternally saved, yet I question whether You care about the minor things affecting me. Please forgive my foolish ways and allowing anxiety to steal my joy by tempting me to question Your plan and purpose for my life. Amen.

CHAPTER 7

Help! I Am Fearful

(I'm tired of feeling trepidation in my heart.)

Fear is a powerful emotion. It can motivate our hearts or stifle our minds, promote positive change and accountability, or leave us paralyzed with doubt and anxiety. Fear has the unique ability to be just as good (godly fear) as it is bad (worldly fear) depending on how we consider it. Discerning between godly fear and worldly fear is critical to survive the seasons of trials we face. We must determine who or what we are afraid of, why we are fearful in the first place, and how we will react or respond based upon our respective fears.

Scripture exhorts us to fear the Lord because He is righteous and holy, author of all Creation, and worthy of admiration and respect. He is omniscient, sovereign, and all things are subject to His authority, power, and dominion. Godly fear is universally dependent on exuding reverence before Him. That is why our posture must be humble, respectful, submissive, and worshipful, rather than naïve, indifferent, or self-exalting. Failing to fear the Lord would be absolutely foolish on our part.

"The fear of the Lord is the beginning of knowledge; fools despise wisdom and instruction."

On the opposite extreme, lack of godly fear magnifies pride and arrogance. It shows how dismissive we are of God's grace, mercy, and blessings which He lovingly pours out on us. While unbelievers dismiss any need for godly fear, those who profess themselves as followers of Jesus Christ should know better. How then do we maintain a healthy dose of godly fear when trials and tribulations tempt us to be consumed by fear of the world? The answer lies in whom or what we ultimately place our faith, hope, and trust for salvation.

The essence of saving faith is putting our trust in God and His sovereign Word. None of us were present when the books of the Bible were written. Therefore, a personal choice must be made whether we refute, question, or believe the validity of Scripture and what the Bible teaches. Keep in mind, there is a significant difference between general faith and saving faith. Far too many Christians have no issue believing God exists, but endorsing the Bible cover-to-cover is a whole different issue. We can believe what the Bible says is true, but if push comes to shove, are we willing to stake our lives on its inerrancy and endure persecution to defend its position?

Perhaps more pointedly, are we willing to surrender all, even our lives unto death, if necessary, rather than reject Christ? Many martyrs came face-to-face with that critical life or death decision. Threatened by accusers to renounce their faith in Christ or suffer torture, imprisonment, or execution, many born-again Christians boldly transitioned from this life to the next resolute in their confession of faith in Jesus for salvation. Personal conviction in the inspired inerrancy of holy Scripture empowered them to risk everything they held dear because God's Word became their source of absolute truth and strength.

The sad truth is very few of us have experience being persecuted for our faith. Most of us live in nations which allow us to worship God freely. Therefore, we struggle understanding what it feels like to endure immense pain and suffer for the Gospel like others across the globe. It is a blessing that Christianity is widely accepted in our world today, but it should also compel us to have cause for concern if we have not experienced persecution for defending God and His Word. Persecution is not something we should aim to avoid. Rather, we must embrace it because Jesus promised His followers that opposition would come to those who proclaimed the Gospel of salvation.

"Blessed are you when people hate you and when they exclude you, revile you, and spurn your name as evil, on account of the Son of Man! Rejoice in that day, and leap for joy, for behold, your reward is great in heaven; for so their fathers did to the prophets."

— Luke 6:22–23

"Blessed are you when others revile you, persecute you, and utter all kinds of evil against you falsely on my account. Rejoice and be glad, for your reward is great in heaven, for so they persecuted the prophets who were before you."

— Matthew 5:11–12

We must also recognize that millions of Christians throughout the past 2,000 years have willingly sacrificed their lives to preach the Word and preserve Biblical manuscripts so we could know God's heart for His people. In many ways, martyred blood paid the ransom for many religious freedoms we enjoy today. Like diving upon a grenade and willingly accepting death, martyrs throughout the ages have sacrificed their safety and well-being to protect and preserve the Bible for future generations. How then could we ever take their gift for granted and avoid defending God's Word because of worldly fear?

What are we so afraid of in this world? Are we not assured of final victory if we claim the name of Jesus as our personal Lord and Savior? Who has the power to crush our spirit other than God since He chose to sacrifice His beloved Son on our behalf? Jesus ransomed the grave and defeated sin once and for all through His death, burial, and resurrection. Whom then shall we realistically fear in this world other than the Lord? He who spoke the world into existence is powerful enough to handle any issue we face, so why are we afraid of tomorrow? Is God not big enough to rescue us from calamity or do we assume He does not care?

> *"The LORD is my light and my salvation; whom shall I fear? The LORD is the stronghold of my life; of whom shall I be afraid? When evildoers assail me to eat up my flesh, my adversaries, and foes, it is they who stumble and fall. Though an army encamp against me, my heart shall not fear; though war arise against me, yet I will be confident."*
>
> *— Psalm 27:1–3*

The problem for most Christians is that we are caught in an identity crisis of epic proportions. We do not know who we are or to whom we belong. We think we exist to please ourselves and pursue ease and happiness as our primary goal in life. However, self-serving motivations leave us longing for more. We expect a mirage to quench our insatiable thirst for fulfillment when only God is adequate to fill our desire for peace and contentment. Truly, we have become spiritually blind to our own blindness when we forget that Jesus paid the ransom for our salvation. How then can we continue to forget who we are in Christ?

"For everyone who has been born of God overcomes the world. And this is the victory that has overcome the world—our faith. Who is it that overcomes the world except the one who believes that Jesus is the Son of God?"

— *1 John 5:4–5*

I can attest that personal sin has a way of putting godly fear and worldly fear into perspective. When I was once enslaved to pornography and appeasing my fleshly desires, godly fear was not on my radar. I felt guilt and remorse for yielding to temptation and looking at women with lustful intent, but my faith did not compel me to quit my addiction. God's Word was not entrenched in my heart, so it was easy to take the Lord's forgiveness for granted and continue feeding my mind with lustful images. Those fallacies only plagued my marriage and inevitably caused me to reject the vows I pledged to my wife on our wedding day due to unrealistic expectations.

I regret that worldly fear consumed me. Foolishly, I was far less afraid of God's impending judgment and completely focused on the aftermath of getting caught. That is why I hid my sins for so long because I did not want to own the consequences of my actions. I wanted to leave them as a conversation between God and I on judgment day because I was scared of the severity of my wife's reaction. Hiding was simply easier, so I kept silent rather than admitting my sins. Eventually, God gave me opportunity to confess and it changed my life forever.

In that moment of confession, I remember being gripped with the enormity of what I had done. My sins caused a tidal wave of destruction in the heart and mind of my wife. In many ways, her reaction affirmed why I had been so fearful to tell her the truth. She was devastated and angry (and rightfully so). However, she was just as fearful as I was but for completely different reasons. My fear was based on the consequences of my actions and potential for divorce. Her fear was whether she could forgive and trust me again. Thankfully, she found the strength she needed in Christ to walk the path of marriage restoration with me, but that was only because she put her faith and hope in God alone, not me.

If we are born again, we are new creations in Christ and no longer slaves to our flesh where worldly fear resides. We are set free from self-reliance to overcome fear in exchange for peace, joy, and contentment through God's sovereign provision. Thus, if we allow stress and anxiety to consume our emotions and drive us into a state of worry and depression, what does that inevitably reveal about our faith in Jesus? Even if we have sinned grievously, does that mean God has abandoned us? Absolutely not! Jesus is with us wherever we go. Therefore, we must cast our fears upon Him so that He can help us live in the light of grace rather than the dark shadows of worldly fear.

"Consider the ravens: they neither sow nor reap, they have neither storehouse nor barn, and yet God feeds them. Of how much more value are you than the birds!"

— Luke 12:24

"Consider the lilies, how they grow: they neither toil nor spin, yet I tell you, even Solomon in all his glory was not arrayed like one of these."

— Luke 12:27

Psalm 46:1-3 reminds us that nothing can separate us from the love of Christ. Why then do we fear all the calamities this world has to offer? Keep in mind, mountains are only moved if the Lord allows, and we are wise to recognize that the mere mention of

His name can cause them to crumble if He wills. Why then do we disbelieve His divine power and majesty? He spoke creation into existence in six days, so why would we trust ourselves more than Him? Is He not infinitely more powerful, knowledgeable, and beyond compare? How can we be more fearful of man than the Lord?

"God is our refuge and strength, a very present help in trouble. Therefore we will not fear though the earth gives way, though the mountains be moved into the heart of the sea, though its waters roar and foam, though the mountains tremble at its swelling."

— Psalm 46:1–3

Far too often, we attempt to place God in a box. We believe we can manipulate His actions and sway His mind to our personal will. What we fail to realize is the more we lean on our own understanding, the more we squeeze Him out from speaking truth into our hearts and minds. If we could step back and view our lives from His holy perspective, we would recognize how foolish we are to assume we know better despite our limited knowledge. Pride does us no favors when we yield to worldly fear. That is why fear of the Lord is the beginning of wisdom, because He is our ultimate source of absolute truth.

"The eyes of the LORD are in every place, keeping watch on the evil and the good."

— Proverbs 15:3

Keep in mind, God's trustworthiness is not based on belief. He is faithful because His promises are true, His love is everlasting, His provision is sovereign, and His sanctification of humanity is pure, holy, and righteous. Though the mountains be moved into the heart of the sea, we will not be shaken because this world is ultimately not our home. That is why death is the great equalizer. It **"separates the sheep from the goats" (Matthew 25:32)** and transitions born-again followers of Jesus Christ from this life to the next where pain, suffering, and worldly fear no longer exist.

"In the world you will have tribulation. But take heart; I have overcome the world."

— John 16:33

Worldly fear only has power over our hearts and minds if we allow. That is why godly fear is critical, because it postures us correctly before the throne of grace so we are safe, secure, and protected from the flaming arrows of the enemy. Nothing good comes from fearing those around us, because worldly fear is meant to magnify our shortcomings in the face of trials and persecution. That is why we must reconcile whom or what we fear most. For when the day of judgment arrives and we stand before God's judgment seat to give account for our lives, nothing but the blood of Jesus will atone for our sinful depravity. Fear of man will be meaningless because godly fear will ultimately convict us when we give account for our lives.

"There is no fear in love, but perfect love casts out fear. For fear has to do with punishment, and whoever fears has not been perfected in love."

— 1 John 4:18

In that moment, judgment will be the only thing we should rightly fear because we can no longer do anything about it. Our time will have run out; our eternal fate sealed forevermore. Therefore, we are wise to reconcile whom we will fear before that day comes. It is sobering to look in the mirror and reflect upon who we have become, but we need not fear judgment if we have reconciled our hearts to God and accepted His gift of salvation. Tomorrow is not guaranteed. So, we are wise to reconcile where we are eternally headed rather than run the risk of not handling our business before judgment day arrives.

Those who are wise recognize the gravity of that decision and have chosen to follow Christ by making Him Lord of their lives. However, those who reject God and demonstrate no fear of His almighty power and majesty will eventually suffer the ultimate consequence. He will cast them from His presence for all eternity to be tormented by unending guilt, shame, and regret for their lack of faith and repentance. Therefore, we must reconcile our hearts back to God and plead with others to do the same. Truly, it is a fearful thing to fall into the hands of a holy God. He is our judge, jury, and executioner on the day of reckoning. Of all the things we should fear, eternal judgment is first and foremost. Nothing else matters because time is of the essence.

"The good person out of his good treasure brings forth good, and the evil person out of his evil treasure brings forth evil. I tell you, on the day of judgment people will give account for every careless word they speak, for by your words you will be justified, and by your words you will be condemned."

— Matthew 12:35–37

"It is a fearful thing to fall into the hands of the living God."

— Hebrews 10:31

Application

1. What are you most afraid of in this world? Why?

2. Why is it critical to distinguish worldly fear from godly fear? What difference does it make?

3. Do you believe God has the power to help you overcome your worldly fears? Why or why not?

4. Why is godly fear the only fear to be deeply concerned about?

5. How has worldly fear over the consequences of your actions stifled your spiritual growth?

6. For those who struggle mightily with worldly fear, why is John 16:33 such a powerful verse to gain proper perspective?

7. If worldly fear magnifies your shortcomings and inadequacies in the face of trials, how can you make necessary changes to demonstrate godly fear instead?

Prayer

Lord, I wrestle with fear daily. It may not be blatantly obvious, but underneath the surface, worldly fear motivates my behavior more than I realize. I tend to look at fear of safety and provision as righteous and use that logic to justify my propensity toward worldly fears. I do not trust Your sovereignty to let go of my fear and accept trials which You allow to test my faith. I often default into needless worry and forget that You are always in control despite my circumstances. Help me die to my fear of man and depend upon Your Spirit to guide my path. You alone are worthy to be feared, Lord, and I will commit my life to trusting Your will rather than subjecting my mind to the enemy's snare. Amen.

CHAPTER 8

Lord, Give Me Protection

(Guard my heart from the enemy's schemes.)

Godly fear is one of the most misunderstood concepts in Scripture. People tend to have too much or not enough, and the lack of clarity around the issue is stifling the spiritual growth of Christ-followers, causing incredible restlessness in countless souls. How then do we fix the problem? The answer begins with determining how to reprogram our minds regarding the fear of God. In other words, we must refocus our attention on reverence which undergirds our personal relationship with Jesus and protects our minds from yielding to worldly fear.

Reverence is a word rarely used in our culture today because of its religious connotations. It constitutes having respect and esteem for positions of power and authority, yet we tend to only hear it referenced in church. Reverence feels a bit old-fashioned or culturally irrelevant to our personal preferences, which is likely why we tend to make light of it. However, godly reverence is the spiritual key which unlocks our hearts and minds to experience the power and majesty of God's holiness. It begins with kneeling before the cross of Christ and humbling ourselves so we can approach the throne of grace on judgment day confident of our eternal fate.

"Therefore let us be grateful for receiving a kingdom that cannot be shaken, and thus let us offer to God acceptable worship, with reverence and awe, for our God is a consuming fire."

— Hebrews 12:28–29

Without question, we are wise to revere God's almighty power and authority for countless reasons, but mainly because He spoke creation into existence and reigns supreme forevermore. From the dust of the earth He created humanity, and to the dust of the earth we will one day return according to His divine providence. How often, though, do we stop and recognize God's power and majesty when we flippantly disregard His wrath and judgment of sin? Or, on the opposite extreme, are we rightly fearing the Lord if all we focus on is His wrath without any mention of His love and grace?

Correctly posturing our fear of the Lord cannot be understated, for most people lean too heavily on the extremes of God's wrath vs. His love without maintaining a healthy balance between both aspects of His character. Having a proper understanding of godly fear is contingent upon first revering His Word as inerrant, absolute truth. In other words, God will not open the floodgate of His knowledge and wisdom if we do not respect Him and trust that His Word is true. A humble and reverent fear of the Lord must be the foundation our faith is built upon because it shapes our personal doctrine regarding ethics, morality, and personal character.

"The fear of the LORD is the beginning of wisdom, and the knowledge of the Holy One is insight."

— Proverbs 9:10

Case in point, far too many self-proclaimed Christians have no clue what fear of the Lord looks like because they have never taken time to read the Bible cover-to-cover. It is easy to celebrate what Scripture says about salvation, yet many struggle accepting what the Bible teaches regarding God's wrath and judgment of sin. As a result, we have no problem with God's love and Jesus accepting the penalty for our sins. We would rather just pick and choose what makes us feel happy than embrace the reality of what Scripture teaches about judgment altogether.

"For God so loved the world, that he gave his only Son, that whoever believes in him should not perish but have eternal life. For God did not send his Son into the world to condemn the world, but in order that the world might be saved through him."

— John 3:16–17

When it comes to God's wrath vs. His love, people often lean toward one extreme or the other without understanding what the Bible says from Genesis to Revelation. The totality of Scripture encapsulates who Jesus is, why He came, and what our relationship to Him as Lord and Savior entails. Therefore, our respect and reverence for the sacrifice He made for the forgiveness of sins should be more than enough reason to trust His Word entirely. Christ died in our place to save us from God's eternal wrath, not because we were worthy of that gift in any way.

"For while we were still weak, at the right time Christ died for the ungodly. For one will scarcely die for a righteous person—though perhaps for a good person one would dare to die—but God shows his love for us in that while we were still sinners, Christ died for us."

— Romans 5:6–8

Psalm 34:7 offers a glimpse into the depth of God's love by protecting us from the snares of the enemy which seek to destroy our faith in Christ. Keep in mind, there are instances throughout Scripture where God sends angels to perform a certain act or give a specific message. However, we cannot expect God to send us divine intervention at every turn to influence and guide our decision-making. He gave us the Holy Spirit instead. Therefore, we are wise to recognize that His protection is unconditional for those who surrender to His authority, trust His Word, and submit to His sovereign will.

> *"The angel of the LORD encamps around those who fear him and delivers them."*

> — *Psalm 34:7*

What we must glean from Psalm 34:7 is there are spiritual forces all around us, good and evil, waging war in ways we cannot see nor comprehend. However, we should feel comforted knowing God provides deliverance from our enemies to those who revere and call upon His name for salvation. The book of 2 Kings provides an outstanding example of how God protects within the spiritual realm. Surrounded by an enemy poised to lay siege on God's anointed prophet, Elisha prayed that his servant's eyes be opened to witness the angelic army which surrounded them. God provided all the divine protection they needed. The servant just needed to open his eyes and recognize it.

> *"When the servant of the man of God rose early in the morning and went out, behold, an army with horses and chariots was all around the city. And the servant said, 'Alas, my master! What shall we do?' He said, 'Do not be afraid, for those who are with us are more than those who are with them.' Then Elisha prayed and said, 'O LORD, please open his*

eyes that he may see.' So the LORD opened the eyes of the young man, and he saw, and behold, the mountain was full of horses and chariots of fire all around Elisha."

— 2 Kings 6:15–17

What 2 Kings 6:15–17 proves is that God's sovereign protection in the spiritual realm far exceeds anything we can imagine. He goes before us in ways we do not comprehend and sees what we fail to recognize. Therefore, we should not fear the enemy's power when he attempts to enslave us but know we are set free from the bondage of sin and death by the blood of Christ. Jesus overcame evil when He died in our place and rose again, and we are called to live for a higher purpose and calling because He paid our eternal ransom.

Recently, my family had the unique opportunity to see God's physical and spiritual protection on display. On December 9, 2023, our house took a direct hit from an EF2 tornado. It only lasted twenty seconds, but our back porch was destroyed and roof damaged (among other things) by the 130-mph winds which encircled our house as it passed over. I had never experienced a tornado firsthand but the roar of the wind is forever etched in my memory. In that moment, we understood how helpless we were to prevent death from impacting our family. However, God spared our lives and home because it was not His will that we should die or that our home be completely destroyed.

There are two things that struck me in the aftermath of the tornado. First, a double-pane window blew out and shot glass all throughout our living room and kitchen, but it was an inside window off our back porch. Once the tornado had passed, heavy rain ensued which could have caused far greater damage inside had the window been on an exterior wall rather than interior. Second, we had pulled the blinds before the tornado hit and those blinds prevented glass from doing far more damage inside our home than it did. Granted, we found glass in our furniture, rugs, and everywhere else, but the bulk of the shards stayed near the window to make the cleanup manageable and damages less expensive to repair.

In our minds, God's sovereign hand of protection was all over us. Not only did he spare our lives but the damages to our house were arguably in the best possible places to keep our home livable during the restoration process. Regrettably, others were not as fortunate as people died in the aftermath. Homes were damaged far worse than what we experienced. I sometimes wonder why we were spared far greater tragedy, but then my mind recalls the moment the tornado roared around our house as we huddled together in the center of our home.

My three daughters who were with us that night were scared and crying out to God for protection, but it was my 8-year-old's reaction I remember most. Considering the dire circumstances, the logical prayer in a tornado would be, "Lord, save us!" That was not what my daughter prayed, though. She was crying out with eyes closed and hands clasped, "Satan, you cannot have this house!" In that moment, her mind was laser-focused on spiritual warfare, and she saw the tornado as the enemy's way of attacking our family's safety. She also knew God was ultimately in control, and that was evident when she focused her attention on slaying the enemy in prayer and calling down the angels of heaven to protect our family.

"For though we walk in the flesh, we are not waging war according to the flesh. For the weapons of our warfare are not of the flesh but have divine power to destroy strongholds."

— 2 Corinthians 10:3–4

Angels are an interesting topic of discussion within the church. Again, there is great confusion regarding who they are, why they exist, and what acts they perform. Angels are an integral part of God's creation, but we must have a proper understanding of what Scripture teaches about them to not be confused. First, angels exist apart from human beings. There is no Scriptural evidence of a person dying and being reincarnated as an angel—watching over loved ones, helping guard and protect, or even speaking directly to us. Moreover, while it is certainly a wishful sentiment when someone we love passes away, angelic reincarnation is not a Biblically supported doctrine whatsoever.

Second, angels can be good or evil. We typically think of them as being holy, praising and serving God almighty and protecting heaven and the elect. However, Satan is a fallen angel (2 Cor. 11:13-15), though he disguises himself as an "angel of light" to tempt humanity into sinning against God. Therefore, we must be keenly aware that angels exist on both sides of good and evil and guard against placing too much emphasis on them. They serve specific purposes ordained by God to accomplish His will, not ours, which is why we respect their power and position in the grand scheme of God's creation.

"Bless the LORD, O you his angels, you mighty ones who do his word, obeying the voice of his word!"

— Psalm 103:20

"For he will command his angels concerning you to guard you in all your ways. On their hands they will bear you up, lest you strike your foot against a stone."

— Psalm 91:11–12

Third, angels of the Most High God are messengers who are worthy of our reverent fear, not based on who they are but who they represent. They communicate on specific occasions for unique purposes. Look no further than the events surrounding Jesus' birth (Mary's visitation, Joseph's dream, and shepherds keeping watch) as well as His resurrection (the empty tomb and Jesus' ascension) as prime examples. However, experiencing an angel firsthand is a rare occasion. We have limited examples in Scripture where angels made an appearance to humanity. That does not mean visitations cannot happen. It simply means we should not expect them.

"When the Son of Man comes in his glory, and all the angels with him, then he will sit on his glorious throne. Before him will be gathered all the nations, and he will separate people one from another as a shepherd separates the sheep from the goats. And he will place the sheep on his right, but the goats on the left. Then the King will say to those on his right, 'Come, you who are blessed by my Father, inherit the kingdom prepared for you from the foundation of the world."

— Matthew 25:31–34

"Then he will say to those on his left, 'Depart from me, you cursed, into the eternal fire prepared for the devil and his angels.'"

— Matthew 25:41

As Christ-followers, we can expect that if we cling to the Lord for refuge and strength and revere His holy name, we can rest assured His angels are encamped around us (just as they were for Elisha) and will protect us from the enemy. In the same token, we must take the Bible seriously and not dismiss a single verse out of context due to ignorance, discomfort, or conviction. Rather, we can trust its inerrancy and all-sufficiency for our lives because minimizing Scripture in any way would only undermine and discredit our faith, rendering us foolish.

God has provided all the wisdom we need to teach us how to protect our hearts and minds. Therefore, we can unconditionally trust Him because we know His intentions are pure. That is why survival this side of heaven begins with posturing our hearts in reverence before our sovereign Creator. The time will come when we will bow before Him on judgment day, and those who obeyed His Word and displayed godly fear during their lifetime will spend eternity in heaven. We know this to be true because the Bible teaches us to be on guard and adequately prepared for our day of reckoning.

"And Jesus cried out and said, 'Whoever believes in me, believes not in me but in him who sent me. And whoever sees me sees him who sent me. I have come into the world as light, so that whoever believes in me may not remain in darkness. If anyone hears my words and does not keep them, I do not judge him; for I did not come to judge the world but to save the world. The one who rejects me and does not receive my words has a judge; the word that I have spoken will judge him on the last day.'"

— John 12:44–48

Those who have chosen a different path and rejected salvation through Christ will give account for their unbelief one day. Sadly, they will be condemned to eternity in hell on account of the poor choice they made to reject the Gospel of salvation. That is a cold and harsh reality we must accept but an expectation we can rely upon as well. Therefore, let us be wise and decide whom we will serve before that day comes, for our eternal choice will determine our future path and how we will spend the remaining time God has graciously given to reconcile our hearts back to Him.

Application

1. When you pray, what type of protection (physical, emotional, psychological, or spiritual) do you ask God for most? Why?

2. What role does reverence play in demonstrating godly fear?

3. Considering God's holy character (wrath vs. love) how do you see Him? Which aspect does your mind gravitate toward and how has this impacted your view of Him as heavenly Father?

4. Give an example where God sovereignly protected you. How did He make Himself known in a miraculous way?

5. What difference does it make knowing God protects you in the spiritual realm far more than you realize?

6. What is your opinion of angels and what role do you believe they play in your life (if any)?

7. Why should spiritual protection always be your #1 concern?

Prayer

Lord, I often pray for Your sovereign protection but am far more concerned with physical needs than shifting my perspective toward the spiritual realm. I know Satan is real. I just do not think about spiritual warfare enough to drive me into Your Word daily for wisdom and discernment. I lean upon my flesh to protect me rather than You, even though I know I am powerless to defeat the enemy in my own strength. Help me rely upon Your Spirit to illuminate my mind with grace and truth. I can easily get lost in the wilderness of my mind and assume I am all alone, but I know that is a lie. You are always with me and I thank You for never abandoning me in my hour of need. Amen.

CHAPTER 9

Help! I Am Weary
(I'm sick and tired of being sick and tired.)

Are we not incredibly tired these days and worn out from the busyness which has consumed our lives? It seems most of us are exhausted to the brink of hopelessness and despair because we are stretched too thin and pulled in countless directions by anything and everything under the sun. How do we remedy the problem and experience physical, emotional, psychological, and spiritual revival in our hearts and minds? How do we find rest for our tired and weary souls before it is too late? The last thing we want to do is crumble under all the pressure we are facing. What then must we do to survive so we avoid throwing in the towel altogether and give up on the hope of tomorrow?

"He gives power to the faint, and to him who has no might he increases strength. Even youths shall faint and be weary, and young men shall fall exhausted; but they who wait for the LORD shall renew their strength; they shall mount up with wings like eagles; they shall run and not be weary; they shall walk and not faint."

— Isaiah 40:29–31

Isaiah 40:29 provides a firm foundation for why we trust in the Lord. Verse-31 reminds us, amid our weariness and fatigue, to look upon Him as our source of strength and power when we feel as if we cannot take another step or make it another day. He is our portion, satisfying the desperate need of our souls in seasons of trial, yet sometimes we do not want to hear what God has to say because we are too tired to listen and heed His wisdom. We are distracted by the storms surrounding us and have no desire to hear logic or reason.

When our emotional tanks are virtually empty, we are running on fumes and bound to stop functioning properly. Our minds are overwhelmed to the point where Biblical truth has no avenue to break through the clutter of distractions. In those moments, what we need is to expel doubts, fears, worries, and frustrations which are fueling our struggles. We need a sustainable source of fuel that never runs dry which can only be found in the absolute truth of Scripture. However, what if we simply have no desire to hear what the Lord has to say? What then?

It is not that we fail to value Scripture as life-giving power when faced with difficulties. As Christians, we know we should respond to trials with joy by trusting God, but oftentimes we are tired of riding a never-ending, emotional rollercoaster which tempts us to lash out from sheer exhaustion and desperation. Fatigue often impairs our judgment, enslaving us to feelings and emotions rather than compelling us to use self-control and take every thought captive for Christ. That is why we must always be on guard and protect our minds from succumbing to weariness.

"A man without self-control is like a city broken into and left without walls."

— Proverbs 25:28

Truly, many of us are at a spiritual crossroads where if people tell us, "You just need to trust God!" we are liable to hurt them because we do not want to hear encouraging words of wisdom. What we want is a sounding board or punching bag to release the pent-up stress we have been carrying far too long. However, if we could shift our perspective and consider fatigue as an opportunity to draw closer to the Lord, we would be less concerned with avoiding a nervous breakdown and more focused on discovering God's grace and peace through the trials we face.

The quintessential fountain of wisdom on the topic of finding strength and rest is found in Matthew 11:28–30, which reminds us to exchange our worldly struggles with the yoke of being a disciple of Jesus. For those who trust Him, the Lord promises freedom from anxiety and the troubles of this world. When we read a passage like this, our flesh tends to reject it as too good to be true. Human reason and logic take over and we think, "How could God literally change my circumstances right now?" Yet despite our doubt, Jesus waits patiently until we are willing to relent our selfish pride and try again His way.

"Come to me, all who labor and are heavy laden, and I will give you rest. Take my yoke upon you, and learn from me, for I am gentle and lowly in heart, and you will find rest for your souls. For my yoke is easy, and my burden is light."

— Matthew 11:28–30

Our biggest problem with rest is that we do not plan for it. It is simply a byproduct of our daily schedules. If time allows, we will rest. If not, we will continue getting used to being tired which only exasperates our problems further. Is that what God wants, though? Does He take pleasure watching us grind through life devoid of peace, feeling like all hope is lost, and assuming our prayers will never be answered? Certainly not! He wants us to rest in Him because He understands our need to cry on His shoulder before receiving salvation to rescue us from mental, emotional, and spiritual bondage.

God wants us to let go of our burdens and take His yoke upon our shoulders instead. He waits patiently for us to exchange our yoke of slavery to fear, doubt, and worry (which binds us to this world) for one that promises eternal freedom and produces peace and contentment. That is why rest is so critical to break the monotony of stress and anxiety in our lives. For by shifting our perspective and prioritizing quality time with God, we can emotionally purge what plagues our minds so our hearts have ample room to receive the promises of His absolute truth.

> *"This Book of the Law shall not depart from your mouth, but you shall meditate on it day and night, so that you may be careful to do according to all that is written in it. For then you will make your way prosperous, and then you will have good success. Have I not commanded you? Be strong and courageous. Do not be frightened, and do not be dismayed, for the LORD your God is with you wherever you go."*
>
> *— Joshua 1:8–9*

The challenge is that when trials crash like a tidal wave upon the shore of our minds, we become psychologically overwhelmed and feel as if we are drowning without any chance of survival or rescue. Granted, the enemy would love nothing more than to capsize our faith with anxiety and turn our lives upside down, but we cannot let him. We must hold firm to the anchor of God's Word which steadies our faith and stops us from being tossed aimlessly by the storms of life. How then do we let go of all things weighing heavily on our minds and trust the Lord amid our fear and doubt?

King David struggled similarly. Despite being a man after God's own heart (1 Sam. 13:14), David wore his emotions on his sleeve and left no stone unturned voicing his unfiltered thoughts and opinions to the Lord about his difficult circumstances. The boldness of his outbursts and accusations are striking. How could he speak to the Lord like he did and not be struck dead? David's emotions mirror how many of us feel when we assume God is distant from us in our hour of need. We often lash out in anger and frustration without recognizing who stands beside us in the fire and ensures we do not get burned.

"My God, my God, why have you forsaken me? Why are you so far from saving me, from the words of my groaning? O my God, I cry by day, but you do not answer, and by night, but I find no rest."

— *Psalm 22:1–2*

Despite David's emotional outbursts (Psa. 22:1–2), he always managed to immediately counter his emotions with Biblical truth (Psa. 22:3–5). He continually washed his mind with the promises of Scripture as a means of protecting his heart from losing faith in God's sovereign provision. His example should encourage us mightily because the Lord is longsuffering when we question His sovereignty. Also, He is not easily offended as we might presume but waits patiently to see whether we will camp out in the valley of despair or shift direction and preach the Gospel to our hearts to embolden our faith.

"Yet you are holy, enthroned on the praises of Israel. In you our fathers trusted; they trusted, and you delivered them. To you they cried and were rescued; in you they trusted and were not put to shame."

— *Psalm 22:3–5*

The remedy to weariness is not swallowing our emotions or keeping busy enough to avoid our problems. We are empowered to pour out our feelings and lay them at the foot of the cross where reconciliation and atonement are found. The longer we allow negative feelings to fester, the more enslaved we become to hopelessness and depression. For if frustration has no means to escape our minds through prayer, there is no remedy to purge our hearts from the deadly poison of anger and bitterness which destroys us from within.

God wants us to cry upon His shoulder, so long as our faith is not shaken but affirmed in the process. His goal is not to drown out our emotions or deem our feelings as insignificant. Rather, He allows us to purge our hearts of negativity and make room for spiritual renewal in return. That is why tears are often a healthy means to an end for those who are lost and hurting. They allow us to release emotions which need to be set free. Tears are God's medicine for the heart and soul because they draw us out of the ashes and give us permission to express our thoughts and feelings without any need for words.

"Those who sow in tears shall reap with shouts of joy! He who goes out weeping, bearing the seed for sowing, shall come home with shouts of joy, bringing his sheaves with him."

— Psalm 126:5–6

This is an area where men can learn a tremendous amount of wisdom from women who are naturally geared to express their emotions freely. The challenge is that men are taught by culture to avoid expressing themselves through tears for fear of being labeled as weak. Men typically stuff their emotions and never allow themselves to reconcile how they feel. In contrast, Jesus wept over the death of His beloved friend, Lazarus, because of the impact it had on Mary and Martha, His dear friends. He also wept bitterly over the city of Jerusalem, knowing beforehand how they would vehemently reject His Gospel of salvation for Jews and Gentiles.

"And when he drew near and saw the city, he wept over it, saying, 'Would that you, even you, had known on this day the things that make for peace! But now they are hidden from your eyes. For the days will come upon you, when your enemies will set up a barricade around you and surround you and hem you in on every side and tear you down to the ground, you, and your children within you. And they will not leave one stone upon another in you, because you did not know the time of your visitation.'"

— *Luke 19:41–44*

As a husband and father of four daughters, I can attest that tears flow freely in our home. Physical expression is constant but the ability to properly harness and channel emotions is where my wife and daughters excel. They do not hold back or stifle how they are feeling. They simply emote freely without worrying about how it might be received. In turn, they process how they are thinking and feeling more easily, whereas I tend to stuff my emotions under the guise of exhibiting self-control. However, I am doing myself no favors when I hold my feelings in rather than seeking to articulate them effectively.

Sometimes it feels like I need to hold it all together and keep calm in difficult circumstances, but that is not always the wisest decision. Most of the issues I face in life are non-emergencies, so why do I default to "quiet mode" when it would be easier to share my feelings with words and tears? Over time, I have discovered how liberating it is to share what is on my heart with my family. That does not mean crying is easy when the right situation calls. It simply means I am learning from my family what it means to be a humble, sensitive, and attentive spiritual leader who prioritizes compassion and empathy.

Renewal of the heart comes when we purge our minds of worldly emotions which weigh us down regularly. The more we release our thoughts in a healthy manner, the greater opportunity is provided for the Holy Spirit to fill our hearts with hope, peace, joy, and contentment. The key is not feeling guilty when we question God's purpose for our lives but expressing our thoughts in prayer so our minds can accept what God has in store to teach us. We will never understand the big picture of God's purpose if we are constantly worried about details or questioning why we must endure difficult trials in the first place. He just expects us to trust His sovereignty unconditionally.

We must also never lose sight of the reasons why God allows pain and suffering to enter our lives. Keep in mind, everywhere we go and everything we do has divine purpose. We go no place by accident and God is not absent from our lives for any second. Therefore, the key to survival is not merely weathering the storms which test our faith but discerning why we suffer amid pain and sorrow and comprehending what the Lord intends to teach us through it. We might not understand why we are suffering, but perspective is key to finding peace in the eye of the storm and not leaning on the empty comforts of the world instead.

For example, Charles Spurgeon, arguably the greatest preacher and pastor of all time, endured incredible depression, slander, persecution, and physical ailments which plagued him throughout his ministry. However, Charles understood that his pain and suffering produced humility and dependence on God as his source of strength, which helped him embrace trials joyfully. He understood they were not void of ministerial purpose but rather a means to an end, which far exceeded his comprehension. God had a greater plan in store and Charles accepted his calling.

Similarly, we are charged to look past our present trials and focus on the future where divine revelation is revealed. However, we need to be patient in the process and understand that God's ways are higher than our own. Our seasons of pain, suffering, and sheer exhaustion have a specific plan and purpose which we cannot comprehend. The key is exchanging our yoke of slavery to fear, doubt, and worry for what Jesus offers at the foot of the cross. Trading our sorrows is the gateway to freedom from the chains which bind our hearts. Anything less is bondage to this world. Anything more is pure joy and satisfaction because we have died to self and chosen to live for Christ's glory.

"Therefore, since we have been justified by faith, we have peace with God through our Lord Jesus Christ. Through him we have also obtained access by faith into this grace in which we stand, and we rejoice in hope of the glory of God. Not only that, but we rejoice in our sufferings, knowing that suffering produces endurance, and endurance produces character, and character produces hope, and hope does not put us to shame, because God's love has been poured into our hearts through the Holy Spirit who has been given to us."

— *Romans 5:1–5*

That is an incredible truth we must wrap our minds around to find rest for our weary souls. However, it does not mean God will rescue us from our affliction. He may allow trials to last a lifetime, yet they are not devoid of purpose but intended to grow our faith so we might minister to others who share a similar fate. In the end, freedom from being tired is all about giving God the glory, honor, and praise He deserves despite how weary our souls feel. Thankfully, He does not forsake those who trust His sovereignty but will meet our needs with grace and mercy, even when we fail to comprehend when, where, how, or why in the moment.

Application

1. Who or what is causing your heart and mind to be tired, restless, and weary these days? How so?

2. Why is trusting God and letting go of fear, doubt, and worry so easy to preach but difficult to apply?

3. What is Jesus trying to teach you in Matthew 11:28-30 about casting your cares upon Him in exchange for His yoke?

4. How can you express your emotions more freely (like King David) but wash your mind with Biblical truth thereafter?

5. Do you cry easily? Why or why not? What can you learn from Jesus' example when He wept and mourned with tears?

6. How has pain and suffering you have endured through trials produced steadfastness, humility, and dependency on God?

7. How has God blessed others through your testimony of faith?

Prayer

Lord, I am overwhelmed by Your grace and love. Despite the trials I have faced in my past and present, You have proven faithful in my season of misery. You never pull away when I question Your sovereignty but continue to watch over my restless soul while I struggle with doubt. Thank You for never forsaking me in my hour of despair. I have seen You work mightily throughout my life despite my poor attitude. You have also used my story to bless others which humbles my soul. Help me to never cower in the face of adversity again but trust You unconditionally. My life is nothing without You, Lord, and I never want to leave the safety and security of Your presence ever again. Amen.

CHAPTER 10

Lord, Give Me Revival

(Ignite the Spirit's fire within me.)

How many of us desperately need spiritual revival? Granted, no matter where we are in our journey of faith, we could all benefit from a healthy dose of spiritual awakening to refocus our time and attention on the Gospel of Jesus Christ. However, the pleasures of this world are often too hard to resist when our spiritual disciplines feel dry and barren. The problem is we are typically too busy to schedule time for God yet wonder, "Why do I feel so tired and empty?" If only we would look in the mirror, we would realize that the most pressing obstacle to experiencing spiritual revival is selfish pride.

Revival is all about breathing new life into dead places, and personal faith is one area we need regeneration more than ever to reignite our passion for the Lord. It requires honesty, self-reflection, and vulnerability in its purest form which is difficult to swallow. We may not care to think of ourselves as spiritually dead, but if we stop and evaluate what monopolizes our time and attention, we will quickly find God on the outside looking in. Our days are simply overrun with busyness, packed schedules, and physical exhaustion rather than quality time growing in our devotion to Jesus Christ.

That is not to say everything we spend our time on outside of God is futile. It simply means we are often so distracted by the things of this world that we forget to prioritize God first and foremost in our everyday plans. If only we refocused our efforts on quenching our spiritual appetite, we would find more rest for our weary souls and discover the peace of God we desperately crave. In reality, His love and grace are not difficult to find. We simply need to shift our perspective and invest our time, energy, and resources living for His pleasure rather than our own.

> *"The LORD bless you and keep you; the LORD make his face to shine upon you and be gracious to you; the LORD lift up his countenance upon you and give you peace."*
>
> — *Numbers 6:24–26*

Spiritual revival originates from a genuine hunger and thirst for the Lord to stir our hearts, awaken our minds, and ignite the Spirit's fire within our souls. It signifies our earnest desire for God to start a holy fire within us once again and renew a genuine hunger to know Him more. Spiritual revival is all about rekindling the embers of thankfulness within us which mirrors our salvation decision to follow Christ. It is an opportunity to look back on our conversion of faith and rediscover the joy of our salvation which we lost. Oftentimes, the storms of life distract our attention from spending quality time with the Lord, but what they cannot steal is our joy in Christ.

> *"As a deer pants for flowing streams, so pants my soul for you, O God. My soul thirsts for God, for the living God."*
>
> — *Psalm 42:1–2a*

Undoubtedly, our souls crave personal intimacy with the Lord, yet we often do not know where to begin prioritizing quality time with Him. We are pulled in countless directions by busyness which prompts us to believe we lack the time needed to invest into our spiritual growth, but is that entirely true? Does our greatest problem boil down to a lack of time available, or could it be an issue of prioritization instead? Do we not have the ability to think creatively and carve out time for God in our daily schedules even if we only have a few minutes?

"Look carefully then how you walk, not as unwise but as wise, making the best use of the time, because the days are evil."

— *Ephesians 5:15–16*

If we are honest, our struggle is not about finding time to dedicate to the Lord, because we have no issue prioritizing things which matter most. Our biggest problem begins and ends with treating our spiritual health and well-being as a chore we are expected to do, rather than something we joyfully look forward to accomplishing each day. It all comes down to perspective, as our attitude (positive or negative) determines our spiritual growth or starvation of faith, based on how we view quality time with God and His Word. Therefore, Scripture must transform in our hearts from merely "ink on a page" to life-giving truth which has limitless power to move mountains.

The question we must ask ourselves is whether our spiritual disciplines are burdens we are expected to bear or privileges we are excited to see produce personal growth. Whether we realize it or not, our souls are crying out daily for life-giving truth from God's Word. However, we often ignore our spiritual hunger pangs and starve our bodies instead. Why? We certainly would never dream of depriving ourselves physically for no more than a few days. However, we foolishly assume we can survive on little to no spiritual food whatsoever without the slightest regard for the consequences of our actions. If only we would open our eyes and look in the mirror, perhaps we would finally recognize how severely malnourished and close to death we truly are.

There was once a time in my life when reading the Bible was the furthest thing from my mind. I had no spiritual disciplines to speak of other than attending church on Sundays. My theology and personal doctrine of truth was relative rather than absolute. I held no Biblical worldview because I had not accepted that the Bible was true cover-to-cover. I drifted aimlessly in my faith with no compass to point me on a straight and narrow path. Looking back, it is evident why I struggled with temptation and fell victim to sin so easily. I lacked humility and conviction, and that lapse in judgment led me down a dangerous, winding road of hypocrisy which I deeply regret.

The problem was I had accepted Jesus as my personal Savior, but I brushed aside the idea of making Him Lord of my life. I did not want to be held back or pinned down by a concrete set of rules to live by. I wanted the freedom to yield to my flesh on occasion and indulge in the pleasures of this world. What I actually needed was spiritual revival, and that is exactly what God had in mind when He removed His sovereign hand of protection and gave me the fruit of my desires. He loved me enough to teach me a hard lesson which brought me to my knees in repentance when the scales of deception fell from my eyes and I saw my sin for what it was. I had finally recognized my depravity and was eager to begin anew with fresh eyes and a broken heart.

"Open my eyes, that I may behold wondrous things out of your law."

— Psalm 119:18

Once we have established a genuine hunger and thirst for revival, our focus must shift to the work of regeneration which transforms us from death to new life in Christ by washing our minds with the absolute truth of holy Scripture. Regeneration represents a radical shift in our personal character of catering to love of self and lusts of the flesh to serving God and obeying His commands. It changes our perspective. Psalm 51:10-11 is a prime example of what regeneration looks like because it paints a beautiful picture of a heart stained by sin, cleansed by the power of Jesus' blood, and renewed by the Holy Spirit.

"Create in me a clean heart, O God, and renew a right spirit within me. Cast me not away from your presence and take not your Spirit from me."

— Psalm 51:10–11

When King David penned the words to Psalm 51:10, he recognized the true depravity and wickedness of his sins and how far he had fallen from grace. He knew his fleshly heart was wretched and that only regeneration from the Lord alone could save him from destruction. Certainly, we can all empathize with David's honest admission because his personal failures echo our own. We have all done things we regret in our past. Yet the promise of Scripture is that if we repent of our sins, God will not only forgive our blatant disregard for His Word but also cleanse us from all unrighteousness. He longs to save us from self-destruction, not because we deserve it but because He loves us so much.

"If we confess our sins, he is faithful and just to forgive us our sins and to cleanse us from all unrighteousness. If we say we have not sinned, we make him a liar, and his word is not in us."

— 1 John 1:9–10

Saint Augustine said, "I never have any difficulty believing in miracles, since I experienced the miracle of a change in my own heart." There is something incredibly powerful about that quote because it reminds us of our moment of salvation when the Lord drew us out from the depths of depravity and raised us to new life by the power of His shed blood. Oftentimes, we look around for signs and wonders of God's miraculous power and wonder why He appears quiet or absent in our time of need. We forget about the spiritual markers He has established in our hearts to look back upon at a later date and embolden our faith in times of great need.

What we must understand about regeneration is that the Lord will make all things new to those who wish to be cleansed and spiritually reborn. Our desire must be repentant and pure if we expect to be set free from the chains of sin which bind our hearts. For if we long for spiritual regeneration more passionately than anything else, He will restore the years the locusts have eaten (Joel 2:25) and renew the joy of our salvation. However, we must trust His Word wholeheartedly to see the fruit of that decision played out in our lives.

When we hunger for the Lord and He quenches our thirst with His Word, we are transformed from the inside out and regenerated from death to new life in Christ. At that moment, our lives are no longer enslaved to our flesh but born-again (John 3:1-15). However, what keeps the fire of spiritual revival alive in our hearts for years to come is determined by how steadfast we are in our commitment to the Lord and how firmly we hold to His Gospel message of salvation as our source of strength. Therefore, unwavering commitment to Christ is paramount to spiritual freedom and being reborn by the power of the Holy Spirit.

"I do not turn aside from your rules, for you have taught me. How sweet

are your words to my taste, sweeter than honey to my mouth! Through your precepts I get understanding; therefore I hate every false way. Your word is a lamp to my feet and a light to my path. I have sworn an oath and confirmed it, to keep your righteous rules."

— *Psalm 119:102–106*

David prayed in Psalm 51:10 that God would renew a right spirit within him to keep his heart firm in his faith commitment. He had tasted the filth of his sin and wept in the sorrows of conviction, so much so that he resolved to never return to the depths of his depravity. He remained steadfast and resolute to honor the Lord, and our response should mirror David's. Like Simon Peter jumping out of the boat when Jesus called to him, we must keep our eyes fixed upon Jesus and not concern ourselves with countless worldly distractions which tempt to sink us emotionally, psychologically, and spiritually.

"And Peter answered him, 'Lord, if it is you, command me to come to you on the water.' He said, 'Come.' So Peter got out of the boat, walked on the water, and came to Jesus. But when he saw the wind, he was afraid, and beginning to sink he cried out, 'Lord, save me.' Jesus immediately reached out his hand and took hold of him, saying to him, 'O you of little faith, why did you doubt?'"

— *Matthew 14:28–31*

When we are laser-focused on Jesus and committed in all we say and do to glorify His Name, no matter what wind and waves attempt to destroy us, we will not be moved because our hearts are united. The key is to not waver from our commitment to honor the Lord, because His Gospel is a hill worth dying on. Therefore, we must work to not extinguish the Spirit's fire in our souls, for He has regenerated our hearts and made us alive once again to pursue humility, godliness, and Christlikeness with reckless abandon.

> *"Abide in me, and I in you. As the branch cannot bear fruit by itself, unless it abides in the vine, neither can you, unless you abide in me. I am the vine; you are the branches. Whoever abides in me and I in him, he it is that bears much fruit, for apart from me you can do nothing."*
>
> *— John 15:4–5*

> *"And this is his commandment, that we believe in the name of his Son Jesus Christ and love one another, just as he has commanded us. Whoever keeps his commandments abides in God, and God in him. And by this we know that he abides in us, by the Spirit whom he has given us."*
>
> *— 1 John 3:23–24*

When we filter everything we say and do through the absolute truth of Scripture for wisdom and discernment and align our personal will with the Father's, change happens. The power of the Spirit is magnified and the enemy is forced to flee because victory has already been won for those who are in Christ Jesus. Therefore, we should not fear the flaming arrows of the enemy because our Lord and Savior already extinguished them on the cross of Calvary.

The beauty of declaring, **"Create in me a clean heart, O God, and renew a right spirit within me" (Psalm 51:10),** is that revival must take place in the brokenness of our hearts to find rest for our weary souls. We cannot expect God to do a miracle in our lives if we are not drawn to Him like a moth to a flame. However, the ember of sanctification is an invitation for the refiner's fire to burn away all our impurities of sin. For no man can stand before the judgment seat of God without being purified, which is why Christ's blood must be our saving grace.

"In this you rejoice, though now for a little while, if necessary, you have been grieved by various trials, so that the tested genuineness of your faith— more precious than gold that perishes though it is tested by fire—may be found to result in praise and glory and honor at the revelation of Jesus Christ."

— 1 Peter 1:6–7

Therefore, rather than succumb to our weariness, let us live with fresh perspective. Our prayer should be for the Holy Spirit to lift the scales of deception from our eyes, like Paul on the Damascus road, so we may clearly see our Savior face to face and receive renewed passion and divine purpose for our lives. Revival will only come if we allow the Spirit free reign in our hearts. Hence, we must be ready when His holy fire falls upon us and brings renewal to our weary souls. Only then will we truly find the peace we desperately crave and renewed strength to sustain us until the day we breathe our last and join our Lord and Savior in heaven for eternity.

"Oh! Men and brethren, what would this heart feel if I could but believe that there were some among you who would go home and pray for a revival —men whose faith is large enough, and their love fiery enough to lead them from this moment to exercise unceasing intercessions that God would appear among us and do wondrous things here, as in the times of former generations."

— Charles Spurgeon
"The Story of God's Mighty Acts," July 17, 1859.

Application

1. How would you define what spiritual revival looks, feels, and sounds like? Have you experienced it? Why or why not?

2. Which dead places of your life do you most need revival?

3. How has God made His presence known to you in a powerful way? What spiritual markers resulted from that experience?

4. How has God spoken to you in a still, small voice? If He has not, how can you begin to quiet your spirit to hear His voice?

5. Why is Psalm 51:10-11 a powerful catalyst for spiritual revival and experiencing the Lord's presence every day of your life?

6. What do you hunger and thirst for more than anything else? How can you begin to align your personal will with God's?

7. What role does God's Word play in your life and how can you experience more of Jesus through holy Scripture?

Prayer

Lord, I am amazed by Your love for a sinner like me. I have done nothing to deserve the fountain of grace and mercy You lavishly pour out every day of my life. I am ashamed to say that I desperately long for spiritual revival in my life yet make little to no effort growing closer to You. As always, I expect You to do all the work while I sit back and live my life separate from You. Please forgive my foolish heart and renew a right spirit within me which yearns for more of You. Ignite a relentless passion in me for wisdom and truth. Help me build healthy spiritual disciplines so I no longer stray from Your sovereign will. I long to rest in Your presence all the days of my life, Lord. Amen.

CHAPTER 11

Help! I Am Broken

(I'm tired of feeling overwhelmed by trials.)

Of all the verses in Scripture, Psalm 34:17-18 is one of the most misquoted. Granted, it is a wonderful encouragement to those who are mourning the loss of a loved one, overwhelmed by trials of life, or struggling with anxiety, worry, and depression. However, none of those circumstances speak to the heart of what it truly means, because we filter it through a "what's in it for me" lens rather than a repentant one. The true power of Psalm 34:17-18 is that it refocuses our attention on the Lord and how we distance ourselves from Him when we go our own way. Thus, we must pause and examine the context of this psalm to understand the deeper meaning behind its wisdom and truth.

"When the righteous cry for help, the LORD hears and delivers them out of all their troubles. The LORD is near to the brokenhearted and saves the crushed in spirit."

— Psalm 34:17–18

What is most interesting are the parallels people draw from Psalm 34:17-18 to Jesus' Sermon on the Mount where He taught,

"Blessed are the poor in spirit, for theirs is the kingdom of heaven" (Matthew 5:3). However, what many fail to realize is that another one of Jesus' Beatitudes (Matt. 5:4) more accurately reflects the true meaning behind Psalm 34:17-18, because it emphasizes the blessing which awaits those who grieve, mourn, and repent over their sins. Truly, we will never experience the victory our souls crave until we embrace our brokenness from a humble perspective and allow the Lord to crush our sinful pride.

"Blessed are those who mourn, for they shall be comforted."

— Matthew 5:4

Matthew 5:4 provides a far more accurate picture of what it means to be brokenhearted. It encourages us to own our foolishness and repent of our sins if we desire to receive the comfort of forgiveness and reconciliation with God. Jesus affirmed how blessed it is to humble ourselves and make amends for the pain and sorrow we have caused our Father in heaven and those we love. Therefore, if we desire to glean the true wisdom of Psalm 34:17-18, it is critical that we completely own the consequences of our actions rather than continue to ignore, minimize, or avoid them altogether.

To mourn our sin means we examine our volitional choice to disobey God from His righteous vantage point. It signifies that we recognize and comprehend how our fellowship with Him is broken when we yield to fleshly desires. When we step away from our selfish piety and view our sins from His judgment seat, we allow the Holy Spirit to convict our self-righteous behavior and open our eyes to absolute truth. However, there is a distinct difference between simply being sorry for our foolish decisions and mourning our sins, and that chasm hinges upon what level of grief we are truly experiencing.

"For godly grief produces a repentance that leads to salvation without regret, whereas worldly grief produces death."

— *2 Corinthians 7:10*

Keep in mind, being "sorry" typically conveys that we are disappointed for getting caught and marginally regretful for making poor choices. A quick apology is a decent starting point toward reconciliation and making amends for our sins. However, it is a shallow response because it fails to resonate remorse and contrition deep within our hearts to elicit repentance. Scripture equates being sorry with worldly grief, because it is a band-aid attempt to lessen the consequences of our actions by minimizing decisions we made. Worldly grief does not require the boundary of zero-tolerance. Rather, it is flexible and can withstand multiple slaps on the wrist because the price to be paid is moderate, bearable, and within our budget, per se.

"Like a dog that returns to his vomit is a fool who repeats his folly. Do you see a man who is wise in his own eyes? There is more hope for a fool than for him."

— *Proverbs 26:11–12*

Unfortunately, worldly grief never fixes our addiction to sin. It simply delays our destruction because we are too naïve to believe we have a problem in the first place, and too foolish to put boundaries in effect to cut off the enemy's supply line of temptation. The biggest problem with worldly grief is that we foolishly think we have found a loophole in God's righteous judgment. In turn, we test our luck like a game of Russian roulette in the hope that we can get away with yielding to our flesh one last time. What we fail to realize is the more we succumb to sin and temptation, the more entrenched the enemy's stronghold traps our mind and hardens our heart against the Lord and His righteous Word.

"For a man's ways are before the eyes of the LORD, and he ponders all his paths. The iniquities of the wicked ensnare him, and he is held fast in the cords of his sin. He dies for lack of discipline, and because of his great folly he is led astray."

— *Proverbs 5:21–23*

Godly grief is birthed out of guilt, shame, fear, and regret. It requires that we humble ourselves by seeking reconciliation with others. It is a response which asks, "Will you please forgive me?" rather than a reaction that merely conveys, "I'm sorry!" The pivotal difference between those two postures comes down to a personal choice. When we ask others to forgive our sins, we relinquish control and give them a critical choice to either forgive our offenses or continue to harbor bitterness and resentment.

Asking forgiveness requires humility and gives the offended party a choice to make. It is a transfer of power which allows the offended to cast judgment upon our actions. Conversely, saying, "I'm sorry," is merely a statement which requires no further action. It admits, "I messed up," but gives no opportunity for the offended party to respond to the apology. Thus, we are wise to understand which posture is more beneficial to true reconciliation as humility is the outpouring of godly grief that 2 Corinthians 7:10 encourages us to embrace.

Nowhere is this example more evident than in the behavior of our children. The minute they are playing with other kids and do something wrong, we are quick to make them say they are sorry so all can move on. However, are we making the right choice if we leave it at that and never teach them what repentance looks like? Worldly grief wants us to quickly move on from our sins to avoid punishment, whereas godly grief recognizes the unique opportunity to ask for forgiveness, because we understand how owning our sins builds character through humility.

"Before destruction a man's heart is haughty, but humility comes before honor."

— *Proverbs 18:12*

Godly grief also requires that we turn away from our sins and walk in the light of God's Word. Oftentimes, we think that if we can just stop sinning, everything will be fine. However, remaining idle is not a wise solution either. It simply delays the inevitable and counts down the clock till we relapse into sinful patterns of our former selves. Therefore, we must build spiritual disciplines which help create a new standard of living to draw us closer to Christ. For if we are born-again, we are no longer expected to default into sinful bents. God has redeemed our hearts, minds, and souls through the blood of Jesus and cleansed us from all unrighteousness.

"Put off your old self which belongs to your former manner of life and is corrupt through deceitful desires and be renewed in the spirit of your minds to put on the new self, created after the likeness of God in true righteousness and holiness."

— *Ephesians 4:22–24*

If we consider the context of Psalm 34, we will find a distinct emphasis on the righteousness of man which is grounded in surrender, obedience, and submission to the Lord for salvation. It is certainly a psalm of praise and thanksgiving to God for His deliverance during seasons of trials and suffering, but we cannot overlook one simple fact which Psalm 34:18 hinges upon. What makes a man truly righteous before God is not contingent on all the good works he has done, but his saving faith in Christ which causes him to respond to the Father in reverence, humility, and repentance when he has sinned. He recognizes his depravity and that only Jesus can save him.

> *"Remember that the man who truly repents is never satisfied with his own repentance. We can no more repent perfectly than we can live perfectly. However pure our tears, there will always be some dirt in them; there will be something to be repented of even in our best repentance. But listen! To repent is to change your mind about sin, and Christ, and all the great things of God. There is sorrow implied in this; but the main point is the turning of the heart from sin to Christ. If there be this turning, you have the essence of true repentance, even though no alarm and no despair should ever cast their shadow upon your mind."*

> — *Charles Spurgeon*
> *"All of Grace," 1885.*

Undoubtedly, we will continue to sin and make foolish choices long after our salvation conversion. This is simply a fact of living in a fallen world and being sinful descendants of Adam and his subsequent fall from grace (Gen. 3). Nonetheless, immersing our hearts and minds in repentance is critical for survival. It is the only gateway to reconciliation and restoration with the Father and freedom from sin which we desperately need. Not that we are planning to fail in the future! Rather, we prepare our hearts to own our sins when that day comes. Our goal is not to minimize, deflect, or blame shift personal responsibility and accountability for our actions. Instead, we must own our sins wholeheartedly.

"Submit yourselves therefore to God. Resist the devil, and he will flee from you. Draw near to God, and he will draw near to you. Cleanse your hands, you sinners, and purify your hearts, you double-minded. Be wretched and mourn and weep. Let your laughter be turned to mourning and your joy to gloom. Humble yourselves before the Lord, and he will exalt you."

— James 4:7–10

When we are crushed in spirit, what is beneath the surface of our hearts eventually comes pouring out (whether we like it or not). Like grapes in a winepress, we expose what is buried deep within us when life's pressures and temptations to sin overwhelm our minds. What we hope to see bursting forth when the walls close in are humility, ownership, self-awareness, remorse, and accountability—the foundational building blocks of genuine repentance. For when we are crushed in spirit, we see what we're truly made of as we seek to own our sins and find rest for our weary souls.

Shepherding men for years, I have seen brokenness play out in many ways. There is a distinct difference between a man who owns his sins and one bent on minimizing the consequences of his actions. It is easy to identify when they begin to tell their stories and pinpoint who is to blame for their foolish decisions. Those who are repentant look deep into the mirror and pull no punches. They call a spade a spade and do not sugarcoat how wretched they were to sin so grievously. There is no avoidance, blame shifting, or justification for their foolish actions. Rather, they accept full responsibility for the decisions they made regardless of who or what influenced them. In other words, they cling to brokenness instead of running away from it because the Lord draws near to the crushed in spirit.

That is why Psalm 34:17-18 is such an incredible passage of Scripture we should always remember, because it reminds us of how close the Lord leans in when we mourn our sins and turn our hearts back to Him. No man who calls upon the Lord in Biblical repentance will be denied his humble request for grace, mercy, and forgiveness. That does not mean we are excused or exempt from the consequences our sins caused, but we are given new opportunities to humble ourselves and learn from our mistakes when those moments of sanctification arise.

"If my people who are called by my name humble themselves and pray and seek my face and turn from their wicked ways, then I will hear from heaven and will forgive their sin and heal their land."

— *2 Chronicles 7:14*

As Christ-followers, we know that our Savior loves us deeply, identifies with our struggles, and is earnestly praying for us just as He did before Peter's denial. He knows we are fallen creatures and will eventually succumb to sin and temptation despite our best intentions to straighten up and fly right. We have been given free will to choose our respective path in life, whether it be to repent of our sin, turn away from foolishness, and walk obediently in the light of His truth, or live in steadfast rebellion. That is why we must remain solely focused on our true north, Jesus Christ, so that we know which direction (heaven or hell) we are ultimately destined for on judgment day.

"Simon, Simon, behold, Satan demanded to have you, that he might sift you like wheat, but I have prayed for you that your faith may not fail. And when you have turned again, strengthen your brothers."

— *Luke 22:31–32*

We can rest assured that the Lord is closer than we could ever imagine, because His Spirit dwells within our hearts—convicting us when we need discipline, guiding us when we crave wisdom, and reminding us that we are born again. We need not fear the enemy when storms of life crash upon the shoreline of our hearts, for we are not slaves to our flesh and expected to yield in defeat. We have been purchased by the blood of Jesus so that our brokenness can be restored, our hearts healed, and our debt paid for all eternity. The Gospel of salvation is not a promise of judgment on the sins of man with no way of escape. God made a way by sacrificing His Son in our place. That is the Good News of the Gospel and we are wise to accept it wholeheartedly.

Therefore, we should boast all the more in our brokenness for that is how the Father draws us unto Himself. We may not particularly enjoy the difficult trials we are destined to face in the grand scheme of our sanctifying journey, but those seasons of trial are designed to teach us incredible truths about who God is and our relationship to Himself. For the Lord disciplines those He loves, and we are wise to let Him prune the dead branches of sin from our lives so we may experience new growth and safe refuge till the day we return home in glory. Only then will we be free from the bondage of guilt, shame, and regret by the power of God's amazing grace.

"But when the fullness of time had come, God sent forth his Son, born of woman, born under the law, to redeem those who were under the law, so that we might receive adoption as sons. And because you are sons, God has sent the Spirit of his Son into our hearts, crying, 'Abba! Father!' So you are no longer a slave, but a son, and if a son, then an heir through God."

— Galatians 4:4–7

Application

1. Which sins in your life are you broken over? Are there any you are struggling to reconcile?

2. How would you differentiate worldly grief from godly grief?

3. When you ask for forgiveness, what are you communicating to those you have sinned against?

4. How has God used your guilt, shame, and regret to draw you unto Himself through repentance?

5. Does hope or despair come pouring out when your mind is exhausted and your spirit crushed? How so?

6. Why is true freedom from sin contingent upon accepting full responsibility for your actions without exception?

7. How have you felt the Lord lean in when you have endured seasons of brokenness in your life?

Prayer

Lord, I am broken. Whether it be through trials, sin, or just life itself, my heart and mind are fragile and in desperate need of repair. Sometimes, I struggle knowing where to begin because all the issues I am facing compound upon one another. The minute I begin to pinpoint one area to fix, others come to fruition and I feel more overwhelmed than when I first started. What I do know is that You draw near to the brokenhearted and save the crushed in spirit, and that is how I feel most days. Help me to stop trying to fix everything myself and lean upon Your Word for wisdom and discernment. Break me of my pride and draw me to the cross where forgiveness, healing, and restoration are found. Amen.

CHAPTER 12

Lord, Give Me Refuge

(Hide me in the shelter of Your wings.)

How often do we look at life from the perspective of glass-half-empty vs. glass-half-full? Do we ever stop and thank God for what He has done for us, or dwell upon what we assume He has not thus far? When we focus our attention on what we lack, we run the risk of complaining and not appreciating what we have graciously been given. However, when we pause and remember how God has infinitely blessed us, we discipline our minds to filter out worry and discontentment by replacing them with joy and thankfulness instead.

"Oh, taste and see that the LORD is good! Blessed is the man who takes refuge in him!"

— Psalm 34:8

Psalm 34:8 reminds us that God is our shelter from the storms of life, protecting us from dangers which seek to hurt us physically, distress which overwhelms us emotionally, and calamity which attempts to destroy us spiritually. We understand the need to run to a safe place during a storm, but do we rest in the security of God's provision when clouds have rolled away and the sun is shining? In other words, is God's protection something we seek only when times are difficult or troublesome, or do we rest in the shelter of His wings all the days of our lives?

"Hear my cry, O God, listen to my prayer; from the end of the earth I call to you when my heart is faint. Lead me to the rock that is higher than I, for you have been my refuge, a strong tower against the enemy. Let me dwell in your tent forever! Let me take refuge under the shelter of your wings!"

— Psalm 61:1–4

We all endure trials which are never planned but consume our focus and attention more than we prefer. It is impossible to anticipate certain trials which tempt us to question why God would allow them to happen, such as terminal illness, natural disasters, or war (just to name a few). In those instances, our faith is stretched much further than we ever dreamt possible. Trials are never easy to accept. How then do we cope with uncertainty in the face of calamity? Where do we run to for safety and security in the midst of the storm? Who will we trust to be our strong tower in times of great need?

"My son, keep your father's commandment, and forsake not your mother's teaching. Bind them on your heart always; tie them around your neck. When you walk, they will lead you; when you lie down, they will watch over you; and when you awake, they will talk with you. For the commandment is a lamp and the teaching a light, and the reproofs of discipline are the way of life."

— Proverbs 6:20–23

The only foundation we should rely upon for wisdom and discernment is God's Word. It is our communication lifeline to God through prayer. We will never know how to respond to trials without Scripture illuminating our path. Therefore, we must reconcile which moral compass will be our guiding light in the darkest hours of our lives. Will we rest on the absolute truth of Scripture which never changes? Perhaps we would rather trust the sinking sand of relative truth which changes frequently and tells us what we want to hear rather than what we need to hear.

"Everyone then who hears these words of mine and does them will be like a wise man who built his house on the rock. And the rain fell, and the floods came, and the winds blew and beat on that house, but it did not fall, because it had been founded on the rock. And everyone who hears these words of mine and does not do them will be like a foolish man who built his house on the sand. And the rain fell, and the floods came, and the winds blew and beat against that house, and it fell, and great was the fall of it."

— Matthew 7:24–27

Far too often, we fail to recognize what a treasure it is to have the heart and mind of God revealed in written form and at our disposal whenever we need. Scripture has become more widely accessible with each passing generation. Yet as time goes on, we have deprioritized its importance in our lives. As a result, we have failed to recognize how Scripture is spiritual food for our souls and critical for survival this side of heaven. Keep in mind, we can survive 3-days without fresh drinking water and 3-weeks without food to eat. However, countless souls starve themselves daily by failing to recognize the endless buffet God has provided. He has freely given us all we need to satisfy our spiritual hunger pangs. Why then do we doubt His refuge?

"Jesus said to her, 'Everyone who drinks of this water will be thirsty again, but whoever drinks of the water that I will give him will never be thirsty again. The water that I will give him will become in him a spring of water welling up to eternal life.'"

— John 4:13–14

If we are honest, our biggest problem is that we fail to equate physical needs with spiritual ones. We compartmentalize the Bible as a survival accessory to our faith journey rather than the trail map itself. Moreover, we trust ourselves and choose to lean on our limited understanding rather than submit to God who is all-knowing and the fountain of wisdom. As a result, we wander aimlessly through life without a care in the world only to wonder how we ended up so hopelessly lost in the process.

"Trust in the LORD with all your heart, and do not lean on your own understanding. In all your ways acknowledge him, and he will make straight your paths. Be not wise in your own eyes; fear the LORD and turn away from evil. It will be healing to your flesh and refreshment to your bones."

— Proverbs 3:5–8

No man willfully chooses to be dropped off in the middle of the most remote and resource-depleted wilderness, content to survive all alone without proper tools, knowledge, and protection from predators and harsh weather. That would be a death trap! Nonetheless, millions of souls die every year, willing and content to starve themselves spiritually than accept the knowledge and wisdom God infinitely provides which can rescue them from any survival scenario. Why then do we reject His help which is readily available? Has He not proven Himself trustworthy?

"There is a way that seems right to a man, but its end is the way to death."

— Proverbs 14:12

It is amazing how stubborn and hardhearted we can be when we choose to veer off course rather than trust God's Word. For the experienced hiker or mountain climber, a trail map is crucial to survival because it protects a man from potential dangers and guards him from committing costly errors which could prove life-threatening. The same is true of the Bible. We have the ultimate survival map readily available to illuminate our path and chart our course. Why then do we trust ourselves more than God during trials? Would we not be more wise to seek His help by reading Scripture for answers?

I cannot begin to count the number of times I leaned on my own understanding and never considered what God had to say. When it came to resisting temptation, I was too proud to ask for help. It was just easier to trust my instincts than consider how futile and short-sighted they actually were. In retrospect, I was like a man lost in the wilderness who attempted to rescue himself. While I could have waited patiently for help to arrive, I chose to hedge a bet on my ability to save myself rather than relinquishing control to God and asking for His wisdom.

For better or worse, I trusted that personal experience and logic were my best option for seeking refuge and maintaining self-control. Sadly, I found myself lost more than ever because I relied solely on my limited strength instead of God's limitless power to provide a way of escape (1 Cor. 10:13). It was not until I humbled myself before God that peace overwhelmed my heart and mind. I learned that I had to remain patient for the Lord to be my refuge and strength.

"But because of your hard and impenitent heart you are storing up wrath for yourself on the day of wrath when God's righteous judgment will be revealed. He will render to each one according to his works: to those who by patience in well-doing seek for glory, honor, and immortality, he will give eternal life; but for those who are self-seeking and do not obey the truth, but obey unrighteousness, there will be wrath and fury."

— *Romans 2:5–8*

In many ways, we often fail to recognize how blessed we truly are. When we find ourselves in dire, survival situations, our first inclination should be to assess what knowledge and resources we have at our disposal before building a plan of action. Far too often, we immediately jump into "fix it" mode when trials arise and rely more on what we think we know rather than asking for God's help. Therefore, if we never spend quality time reading the Bible (knowledge) and meditating on its meaning and purpose (understanding), we will never apply what we have learned and know which path to take in life (wisdom).

What makes the refuge of God so pleasing to our senses is knowing He always has our best interest in mind. All we need to do is take inventory of our lives because His abundant blessings are on full display if we would open our eyes and appreciate what we have been given. Oftentimes, we focus on what we lack and complain about what God is not doing, because we fail to realize He has given us everything we need to survive this world.

When we doubt God's provision, we arrogantly declare that we know better. Rather than thank Him for what He has already done and will continue to do in the future, we dwell on negatives and allow our hearts to grow restless and discontent. We become prone to wander, infatuated with greener pastures which appear luscious and fulfilling. However, the mirage of an oasis will not quench our hunger and thirst. It will only leave us more parched, desperate, and hungry instead of satisfied and fulfilled.

"And let the peace of Christ rule in your hearts, to which indeed you were called in one body. And be thankful. Let the word of Christ dwell in you richly, teaching and admonishing one another in all wisdom, singing psalms and hymns and spiritual songs, with thankfulness in your hearts to God. And whatever you do, in word or deed, do everything in the name of the Lord Jesus, giving thanks to God the Father through him."

— Colossians 3:15–17

Far too often, we fall victim to glass-half-empty perspectives which consume our minds with things we lack. However, when we cling to the Lord as our refuge and safe haven, it does not matter what life throws our way because His grace is always sufficient. His provision is sovereignly perfect. In turn, we recognize the silver-lining of God's grace amid our trials instead of complaining about them. If we have received salvation by grace through faith in Christ, we are more than conquerors and able to withstand the flaming arrows of the enemy which seek to steal our joy and draw us away from God's sovereign protection.

Granted, that does not mean life will suddenly become easy to bear. Trials will continue to test our faith and measure the depth and breadth of our heart's devotion to Jesus as the anchor of our souls. However, contentment is not something we can simply purchase at the grocery store to replenish us when we are running low. It comes only when we choose to accept God's provision despite what the future holds. It is a sacrifice of faith and trust that God is who He says He is in the pages of Scripture and will not abandon us in our hour of need. The Lord intimately knows those who are His, and we are wise to ensure we have reconciled our hearts to Him eternally before it is too late.

"The LORD is good, a stronghold in the day of trouble; he knows those who take refuge in him."

— Nahum 1:7

"I am the good shepherd. I know my own and my own know me, just as the Father knows me and I know the Father; and I lay down my life for the sheep. And I have other sheep that are not of this fold. I must bring them also, and they will listen to my voice. So there will be one flock, one shepherd. For this reason the Father loves me, because I lay down my life that I may take it up again. No one takes it from me, but I lay it down of my own accord. I have authority to lay it down, and I have authority to take it up again. This charge I have received from my Father."

— John 10:14–18

Psalm 34:8 is a powerful reminder of how thankful we should be for the blood of Jesus which protects us from God's wrath and eternal judgment against sin. The grace God provides is so amazing because His wrath against sin is so fierce. Therefore, we must reconcile our souls and trust in Jesus for salvation to avoid spending eternity in hell separated from God's love. Many self-proclaimed Christians have been baited into believing God will let anyone into heaven because His love is unconditional. What they fail to realize is that grace is meaningless without an equal and opposite effect which magnifies its intrinsic value. God's love and wrath are a package deal, not exclusive of one another, which means we must reconcile both to receive salvation.

While it is true that God is love, it is only part of the Gospel story because His love satisfies His wrath. That is why the Father sent His beloved Son to die on our behalf because His holy and righteous law required a blood atonement to cleanse us from all unrighteousness. Apart from our Lord and Savior, Jesus Christ, we are destined to spend eternity in hell, cut-off from our Father in heaven. Without question, the Gospel is stripped of its ability to save us when we minimize or ignore God's wrath in favor of His love. That is why we cannot forget the reason Jesus died—to rescue us from damnation and separation with God the Father for no other reason than unconditional love.

"For while we were still weak, at the right time Christ died for the ungodly. For one will scarcely die for a righteous person—though perhaps for a good person one would dare even to die—but God shows his love for us in that while we were still sinners, Christ died for us. Since, therefore, we have now been justified by his blood, much more shall we be saved by him from the wrath of God. For if while we were enemies we were reconciled to God by the death of his Son, much more, now that we are reconciled, shall we be saved by his life. More than that, we also rejoice in God through our Lord Jesus Christ, through whom we have now received reconciliation."

— Romans 5:6–11

Bottom-line, let us taste and see what the Lord has done and give thanks to God for His sovereign protection when we least deserve it. For the day will come when we will stand before the judgment seat of Christ and give account for our lives, and nothing but the blood of Jesus will satisfy God's eternal wrath against sin. That is why Psalm 34:8 is such a powerful declaration because we give thanks for the safe refuge and security found in the salvation of Jesus Christ. May we never take for granted the eternal sacrifice He made which enables us to reconcile our hearts to Him through godly grief and genuine repentance. For He is our ultimate way of escape from the power of sin and death, and we are forever indebted to Him for willingly sacrificing Himself and dying in our place.

Application

1. What does it mean to take refuge in Christ? How does that manifest itself in your life?

2. Is your perspective more "glass-half-empty" or "glass-half-full" concerning trials? Why?

3. Why is it easier to trust your instincts than ask others or the Lord for help?

4. How quickly do you turn to God's Word for wisdom and discernment in difficult moments? Why?

5. Is the Bible merely a survival accessory or a treasure map you reference daily? Why is that distinction critical to overcoming seasons of trials in your life?

6. How have you doubted God's sovereign provision when your prayers were not answered as you expected? What has God taught you in those seasons of unbelief?

Prayer

Lord, I thank You and praise You for being my rock and my redeemer. Despite the trials I have faced, You have never left my side. You always hear my prayers and give me strength, yet I often doubt whether You will continue to meet my needs. Please forgive my unbelief, Lord. You have never failed me and never will. It is I who have failed You by not washing my mind with the absolute truth of Your Word daily. Give me fresh perspective and an insatiable hunger to know You more. I cannot survive trials if I only rely on personal experience, logic, and reason to save me. Thus, help me die to self and always take refuge in You. Amen.

CHAPTER 13

Help! I Am Tempted

(I'm tired of living for worldly pleasures.)

Have you ever read a passage of Scripture so many times that you think you know what it means? Such is the case with Romans 12:1-2 which compels us to resist the desires of the flesh and cling to God's Word as our source of wisdom in a fallen world. We often hear this passage referenced as a reminder for Christians to hold firm to their Biblical morals and values in the face of evil. It is also a warning for us to separate ourselves from the patterns of this world and focus attention on how God wants us to live. However, do we even know what it looks like to be transformed by the renewal of our minds, or are we just assuming we understand without considering what Paul is teaching to the church of Jesus Christ?

> *"I appeal to you therefore, brothers, by the mercies of God, to present your bodies as a living sacrifice, holy and acceptable to God, which is your spiritual worship. Do not be conformed to this world, but be transformed by the renewal of your mind, that by testing you may discern what is the will of God, what is good, acceptable, and perfect."*

> — *Romans 12:1–2*

Keep in mind, Romans 12:1-2 contains the subtitle, "A Living Sacrifice," because following Jesus demands we live contrary to relative truth which is increasingly prevalent in our society and designed to appeal to our fleshly desires. Relative truth is nothing more than a belief or train of thought which ebbs and flows over time. It holds no permanent, doctrinal value but changes often. In other words, what is true today may not be tomorrow, and what is true for one person may not be for another. Therefore, it is impossible to say anything is morally right or wrong because things can change over time based on opinion, culture, personal experience, or circumstance.

Absolute truth from a Biblical perspective is quite different. It establishes a non-negotiable, zero-tolerance standard regarding ethics and morality, clearly distinguishing right from wrong based on the doctrine of holy Scripture. It warns against the danger of living in opposition to God's holy law. Scripture is intentionally black and white to differentiate sin from righteousness. It helps distinguish those who publicly profess faith in Jesus Christ and the infallibility of His Word from unbelievers who reject the Bible as absolute truth cover to cover. That is why complete faith in the entirety of Scripture is critical, because Jesus cannot be separated from the truth of His Word.

"In the beginning was the Word, and the Word was with God, and the Word was God. He was in the beginning with God. All things were made through him, and without him was not anything made that was made."

— John 1:1–3

"And the Word became flesh and dwelt among us, and we have seen his glory, glory as of the only Son from the Father, full of grace and truth."

— John 1:14

"He is clothed in a robe dipped in blood, and the name by which he is called is The Word of God."

— *Revelation 19:13*

Granted, some may bristle at the notion that unconditional belief in the inerrancy of Scripture is somehow a fine print clause in the salvation contract. However, consider how ridiculous it is to believe what the Bible says regarding salvation yet refute what it says on other issues. If we can reject even one verse of Scripture for whatever reason, then all is invalid because it is no longer absolute but relative. One must believe the Bible is 100% true or reject it altogether, because there is no middle ground on the validity of Scripture from God's point of view. Nevertheless, many people and even church denominations today question the interpretation of Scripture and change its meaning to justify what the Bible clearly defines as sinful behavior.

Look no further than cultural issues such as homosexuality, gender identity, or abortion, which are permeating Christianity and seeking to discredit the Bible. As the body of Christ, we are in a truth war. God will not stand for His Word being disgraced by the deviance of those who seek to redefine its meaning to justify sin. A man will never be saved from damnation if he does not believe what the Bible teaches, so why do we accept evil reinterpretations of Scripture in the church under the justification of inclusion, diversity, or human rights? Are we not lying to unbelievers and loving them to hell itself when we teach that God accepts them just the way they are without a need for repentance?

"The words of the Lord are pure words, like silver refined in a furnace on the ground, purified seven times."

— *Psalm 12:6*

"Every word of God proves true; he is a shield to those who take refuge in him."

— *Proverbs 30:5*

Jesus said, **"Do not think that I have come to abolish the Law or the Prophets; I have not come to abolish them but to fulfill them" (Matthew 5:17)**. Moreover, **"I am the way, and the truth, and the life. No one comes to the Father except through me" (John 14:6)**. Scripture is abundantly clear regarding the relationship between Jesus and His holy Word. Therefore, we are wise to avoid discrediting and disregarding its validity and blunt definition of sin and begin renewing our minds with absolute truth, so we can discern what is good, acceptable, and pleasing in the Lord's eyes.

Before we discern what it means to avoid being conformed to this world, it is imperative we address one issue which most Christians shy away from. Personal judgment is something which can silence most people from expressing their opinions on issues of morality. Cultural opposition has many Christians so scared of endorsing what the Bible teaches that they choose to ignore its truth for fear of persecution. Look no further than the abortion debate where Christians are rejecting Scripture's position on the issue and justifying sin as a legal right rather than a moral concern.

Granted, that does not mean we are called to judge others for false doctrine they mistakenly believe is true. Rather, God exhorts us to make judgment calls within the church regarding what is morally right and wrong based on the absolute truth of Scripture. The caveat to making a judgment call is ensuring we apply what God's Word teaches to our lives, first and foremost, because we cannot preach to others what we fail to practice personally. That would be hypocritical and woefully misleading to others which God will hold us accountable to on judgment day.

"Do not judge by appearances, but judge with right judgment."

— John 7:24

It is critical we eliminate hypocrisy from the equation and welcome the opportunity to be held accountable by God's Word. Far too often, we apologize, excuse, or diminish Scripture to sidestep personal responsibility. However, we cannot allow our minds to justify sin as righteous before God to appease our flesh or protect others from reaping the consequences of their actions. God's law is eternal and He has established a strict standard of righteousness in which humanity must adhere to, whether we like it or not.

"For the wrath of God is revealed from heaven against all ungodliness and unrighteousness of men, who by their unrighteousness suppress the truth. For what can be known about God is plain to them, because God has shown it to them."

— Romans 1:18–19

Nonconformity is a difficult topic to address because the depth and breadth with which we apply God's Word differs from individual to individual. That does not mean God's standard of righteousness changes one iota (past or present). Rather, our position on noncompliance is influenced by personal experience. For instance, if we are exposed to family members who struggle with excessive alcohol consumption, we can either conform to the accepted culture or abstain from drinking. Romans 12:1-2 challenges us to not only abstain out of wisdom but understand why we are doing so. Perhaps it is because alcohol is a personal temptation or maybe we are determined to avoid being a stumbling block to those who struggle with overconsumption.

It could be that drinking alcohol seems foolish or could pose a potential danger if we relinquish self-control, so we avoid it altogether. No matter the choices made, we must always prepare to explain ourselves so that our reasoning draws people to Christ rather than bringing hypocrisy into consideration for our actions. Persecution may come from holding firm, personal standards, but we must answer to God almighty for the judgment calls we make because accountability drives our respective decisions so that we live on mission for righteousness.

"Bless those who persecute you; bless and do not curse them."

— *Romans 12:14*

The challenge is how do we reconcile issues where Biblical doctrine opposes cultural acceptance? Look no further than many hot-button, social issues plaguing our nation which stand in opposition to the Bible's unapologetic, nonconformist stance on what is morally right and wrong in God's eyes. Undoubtedly, society is bent on demonizing Christians and Biblical doctrine as detriments to personal freedom in our culture. Therefore, it is critical we count the cost of following Jesus which includes our universal position on the inerrancy of holy Scripture.

We know that our enemy will not stop until he has eradicated Bible-believing Christians from all authority positions in society. He wants to silence us completely for our faith-based values. That is why we all have an important choice to make. We can either be swept away by the raging current of relative truth, postmodernism, and cultural acceptance, or boldly stand on the Word of God and endure persecution for defending Biblical morals and standards. The choice is inevitably ours, but we must choose wisely or else risk being consumed by the world's cultural ideals altogether.

"And if it is evil in your eyes to serve the LORD, choose this day whom you will serve, whether the gods your fathers served in the region beyond the River, or the gods of the Amorites in whose land you dwell. But as for me and my house, we will serve the LORD."

— Joshua 24:15

What the world does not comprehend is that as unashamed, born-again, Bible-believing, Christ-followers, we consider our temporary sufferings as inconsequential compared to the eternal sacrifice our Lord and Savior made to secure our salvation. That is why suffering for the sake of the Gospel is such a blessing and honor because we recognize how insignificant our sacrifices are compared to what our Lord and Savior endured for our sake. We not only appreciate the gift being given but the one who gave it.

"Beloved, do not be surprised at the fiery trial when it comes upon you to test you, as though something strange were happening to you. But rejoice as far as you share Christ's sufferings, that you may also rejoice and be glad when his glory is revealed."

— 1 Peter 4:12–13

Countless martyrs who willingly shed their blood rather than renounce the name of Jesus as Lord and Savior did so with peace in their hearts knowing they would see Christ in heaven one day. They refused to conform to the pattern of this world but instead, embraced the absolute truth of God's Word as their spiritual nourishment. Similarly, we should not back down nor apologize for what the Bible teaches no matter how intense the opposition we face may be. Scripture is indeed convicting truth, but it is also life-giving freedom to those who place their complete trust in its saving grace and mercy.

To better understand how Scripture can help us discern God's will, let us think of it as a colander one would wash food with and consider how it cleanses our minds with absolute truth. When we read God's Word, we filter cultural beliefs and ideologies out of our minds and refresh our hearts with God's life-giving promises. These further solidify our convictions and reaffirm our faith in Christ because Scripture is the ultimate smorgasbord of choice fruits. Thus, we are wise to understand what blessings await those who put their faith and trust in the Lord alone and the promises of His Word.

"But the fruit of the Spirit is love, joy, peace, patience, kindness, goodness, faithfulness, gentleness, self-control; against such things there is no law."

— *Galatians 5:22–23*

Oftentimes, we fail to filter our hearts' impurities and become lazy in our spiritual disciplines, leaning on limited understanding when we should know better. It is easy to do, especially if our spiritual disciplines of Bible study, prayer, and meditation are lacking. The same holds true if we are spending little to no time applying what we learn for wisdom and discernment. In those moments of self-sufficiency, we fail to recognize how Scripture is meant to nourish us when we are weary and revive us when the schemes of the enemy threaten our lives.

If only we would cling to God's Word as absolute truth, discerning the will of the Father would become much less difficult and far more attainable. We could more easily distinguish right from wrong and not waver in doubt or fear when opposition threatens to attack or persecute us for our belief in Christ. We would know God's absolute truth which sets us free from sin and not succumb to pressure when our culture seeks to discredit our message of salvation in the Lord alone.

"How sweet are your words to my taste, sweeter than honey to my mouth! Through your precepts I get understanding; therefore I hate every false way."

— *Psalm 119:103–104*

The reason so many Christians run away or cower from defending their faith is because they are afraid of persecution. They presume the costs are too great, but who are we to place creature comforts above God Himself? Is He not greater? Jesus died to set us free! May we live in peace, joy, and thankfulness, knowing the victory has already been won. Satan can do nothing to harm us eternally if we are born-again spiritually. Therefore, let our minds be renewed so we no longer live in fear and doubt but humble confidence in the death, burial, and resurrection of Jesus Christ.

"The saying is trustworthy and deserving of full acceptance, that Christ Jesus came into the world to save sinners, of whom I am the foremost."

— *1 Timothy 1:15*

To be a living sacrifice unto the Lord requires we commit to willingly endure attacks from the enemy on all sides and in every direction. In Christ, we no longer fight our own battles. God has already done the work for us because He defeated death on the cross of Calvary and rose from the grave. Thus, let us consider our trials with joy (James 1:2) and hold fast to the absolute truth of God's Word, so that when judgment day comes our Father in heaven will solemnly declare, **"Well done, good and faithful servant. You have been faithful over a little; I will set you over much. Enter into the joy of your master"** (Matthew **25:21**).

Application

1. When you read Romans 12:1-2, which portion resonates most with you? Is it encouraging or convicting? How so?

2. What does being a "living sacrifice" mean to you? Why?

3. How can you find everlasting freedom in the non-negotiable, zero-tolerance standard of holy Scripture?

4. How is your personal faith doctrine dependent upon your standard of truth (relative or absolute)?

5. Why must you believe that Scripture is 100% true or reject it altogether?

6. How are nonconformity and persecution intertwined in the life of a Christ-follower? How can you relate?

7. Are you afraid of persecution? Why or why not?

8. In what ways have you conformed to the pattern of this world and fallen victim to relative truth?

Prayer

Lord, the more I consider how temptation has impacted my life, the more I realize that my standard of truth ebbs and flows with culture to minimize or justify my personal behavior. I am convicted by how easily I have succumbed to watering down my personal faith doctrine to appease fleshly desires. I recognize how critical Your Word is to survive this side of heaven and how steadfast I must be to defend Your absolute truth. Far too often, I cower in the face of persecution instead of boldly defending the inerrancy of Scripture. Please forgive me, Lord. Amen.

CHAPTER 14

Lord, Give Me Escape

(Lead me in path of righteousness.)

When temptation comes knocking at your door, what do you typically do? Do you open to see who knocked or avoid answering and wait for whomever to go away? What if temptation broke through the door and intruded upon your home uninvited? How would you respond? Would you defend yourself and confront the enemy or run and hide because you knew you were helpless to defeat it? It is an interesting debate. On one hand, it could save your life. On the other hand, it could potentially cost you everything if you act recklessly and without discernment.

In many ways, we might rationalize that scenario by saying, "Well, it all depends. How bad is the temptation? Am I equipped to manage it based on my knowledge and skill set? What are the potential risks if I choose to stay and fight vs. cut my losses and run away?" All are valid questions, but are they what we should be asking ourselves? In other words, are we trying to solve the problem based on personal experience and limited understanding, or does God want us to respond differently? We may assume we are strong enough to confront the enemy, but what will we do when we realize that our opponent is more powerful than we initially presumed?

"Watch and pray that you may not enter into temptation. The spirit indeed is willing, but the flesh is weak."

— Matthew 26:41

Temptation is inevitable this side of heaven. No matter how hard we try to live for Christ, temptation always seems to knock at our door. It wants nothing more than to step inside the entryway of our minds and take permanent residence in our hearts to keep us continually enslaved to our flesh. Granted, it does not force its will upon us but baits us into letting it in by appealing to our fleshly desires for ease, pleasure, comfort, and fulfillment. It preys upon weak and selfish pride and convinces us that we are strong enough to know what is best. Truly, it is nothing more than self-deception intended to keep us in bondage even further to our flesh.

That is why we must be diligent to not think more highly of ourselves than we ought or assume we are strong enough to resist sin and temptation on our own. Heaven knows we are powerless to subdue the enemy by ourselves. Our knowledge and personal experience are limited apart from the Lord's sovereign wisdom, guidance, and counsel. Therefore, why would we ever attempt to confront temptation without carefully planning our course of action, contingency plan, and way of escape in the event we find ourselves on the brink of defeat?

"No temptation has overtaken you that is not common to man. God is faithful, and he will not let you be tempted beyond your ability, but with the temptation he will also provide the way of escape, that you may be able to endure it."

— 1 Corinthians 10:13

No soldier steps into a conflict without accurately assessing the terrain and evaluating his enemy's capabilities. He knows that he must properly strategize a wise plan of attack and contingency escape routes in the event of emergency. If he doesn't, he will likely die in battle rather than live to see another day. The same principle applies spiritually. If we have never taken time to plan our offensive and defensive strategies, how will we be properly equipped to endure whatever temptation Satan uses to attack us? That is why training is critical to success because it forces us to plan for any survival scenario we might find ourselves in.

"For which of you, desiring to build a tower, does not first sit down and count the cost, whether he has enough to complete it?"

— Luke 14:28

"Or what king, going out to encounter another king in war, will not sit down first and deliberate whether he is able with ten thousand to meet him who comes against him with twenty thousand?"

— Luke 14:31

Too often, we blindly walk into spiritual warfare and assume we are equipped for battle without putting in the necessary effort to train our minds and defeat the enemy. We believe we know how to defend our minds, but we often become lazy in our spiritual disciplines, spending little to no time in Scripture yet assuming we are prepared for battle each day. What is worse is that we tend to rely more on logic and common sense because they feel more tangible and require less discipline. However, they are not more beneficial to combat spiritual warfare but simply a temporary fix. What we actually need is God's Word because it is our only sufficient means to defend ourselves against the enemy.

"By wisdom a house is built, and by understanding it is established; by knowledge the rooms are filled with all precious riches."

— Proverbs 24:3–4

Personal experience can only get us so far because what looks and feels right might not always be the wisest choice to make, especially concerning temptation. Indeed, personal knowledge is limited, so we cannot lean on common sense and logic to resist temptation. We require something absolute and concrete to bind our hearts to, which is why anchoring our souls to God's Word is key to survival. It shifts the perspective off of us and onto the Lord who is all-knowing, all-powerful, and omnipresent in every situation we encounter.

"Everyone who comes to me and hears my words and does them, I will show you what he is like: he is like a man building a house, who dug deep and laid the foundation on the rock. And when a flood arose, the stream broke against that house and could not shake it, because it had been well built. But the one who hears and does not do them is like a man who built a house on the ground without a foundation. When the stream broke against it, immediately it fell, and the ruin of that house was great."

— Luke 6:47–49

Paul reminds us that no temptation has overtaken our minds that is uncommon to man. That truth should encourage us mightily because our struggles are not unique to us. Oftentimes, we feel all alone struggling through trials or battling a sin addiction, but nothing could be further from the truth. Satan knows full well which buttons to push in our minds because his tactics have not changed since the beginning of time. He has always leveraged his attention on how we feel at any given moment, because we often allow emotions to dictate our actions rather than relying on God's absolute truth for discernment and clarity.

For example, men have a natural tendency to isolate when tired, stressed, angry, frustrated, or overwhelmed. In many ways, it is a defense mechanism to compartmentalize emotions so as to cope with them better. Not to say that is a wise and healthy decision. However, when the trials of life begin to overwhelm our psyche, we often default into self-protection mode and lean on ourselves to fix a particular issue rather than asking for help. Self-preservation takes over our minds and we react rather than wisely respond to maintain some semblance of self-control.

My wife tends to frequently bring this issue to my attention. When the laundry list of things she needs to do compounds, I default into "fix-it" mode and begin taking over tasks without considering her feelings and opinions. In my mind, I am helping by asserting leadership, being proactive, and checking items off her list. However, I am causing division in my marriage because I am no longer collaborating on decisions, big and small. I am just reverting to my former independent bachelor mode, and taking over without any regard for how she thinks and feels. Pride makes me feel as if I know better, so I fall back into isolation mode rather than collaborate together.

"A fool gives full vent to his spirit, but a wise man quietly holds it back."

— Proverbs 29:11

In the moment, recognizing selfish pride can be difficult. Our goal is to manage stress as best we can, but we often do it in our own strength rather than yield to the Holy Spirit. That is also why Biblical community is so vital, because we need the wisdom and perspective of others to identify our blind spots. The body of Christ can point us to Scripture and help correct our behavior when we succumb to temptation. All we must do is humble ourselves and accept accountability.

"Two are better than one, because they have a good reward for their toil. For if they fall, one will lift up his fellow. But woe to him who is alone when he falls and has not another to lift him up!"

— *Ecclesiastes 4:9–10*

We typically avoid personal accountability because we do not want to face the harsh reality of our sins or own the consequences of our actions. Confessing habitual sin or struggles to temptation is a humiliating and emasculating experience. Men, especially, avoid it like the plague. If only we would lay down our pride, we would see that God has placed unique individuals in our path who can help us survive difficult life seasons which are designed to refine our character and strengthen our faith. God does not want us to self-protect and isolate into darkness. Rather, He wants us to live in the light of His unending grace and mercy where true freedom is found.

Where the rubber meets the road comes in our ability to recognize the exit signs God provides and walk in faith towards them. When we are held captive in the darkness of our minds, seeing the slightest glimmer of light at the end of the tunnel can change the trajectory of our lives forever. The key is recognizing what hope looks like and why we should choose it. There are physical ways of escape we can select when we feel temptation beginning to intensify. However, knowing why we are acting on them in the moment is critical to putting a stop gap between desire and action. In other words, we need to know the "Why?" behind our respective decisions if we expect to better prepare for them in the future.

That is the point where physical reality and spiritual maturity intersect. For instance, if a man struggles with lust and wandering eyes, he can learn to bounce his eyes when he sees an attractive woman in the distance. He can guard himself and shift his focus from allowing his mind to wander into a deeper craving for lustful fulfillment through sexual immorality. However, if he does not have a concrete reason why he is escaping temptation in the first place, yielding to sin is virtually unstoppable and likely expected because he has prepared to fail by succumbing to temptation.

"I've made a covenant with my eyes; how then could I gaze at a virgin?"

— Job 31:1

I often exhort men who complete my **"Wilderness Survival, Vol-1 & Vol-2"** discipleship curriculum to wrap their minds around the "moment of decision" as it relates to sin. In other words, when temptation is at its most critical intensity and we are wrestling with the final decision of yielding to our flesh, God's Word must transform from merely ink-on-a-page to life-giving-truth in our hearts and minds. For if we believe God has given us everything we need which pertains to life and godliness, including our way of escape, then we must trust His Word so intensely that the truth of Scripture overpowers our fleshly cravings.

"His divine power has granted to us all things that pertain to life and godliness, through the knowledge of him who called us to his own glory and excellence, by which he has granted to us his precious and very great promises, so that through them you may become partakers of the divine nature, having escaped from the corruption that is in the world because of sinful desire."

— 2 Peter 1:3–4

God's Word is the only permanent way of escape we will ever need in any situation, every moment of our lives. It is the ultimate Swiss army knife of knowledge, wisdom, and discernment which can rescue us from any temptation the enemy throws our way. However, its effectiveness is contingent upon our faith and unwavering trust in its inerrancy, sufficiency, and sovereignty over our lives. Therefore, we must believe without hesitation that it is applicable to every situation we will encounter this side of heaven, because like it or not, our survival depends upon it.

It might not seem like trust in God's Word is the way of escape we have ultimately been searching for, but it is. Tangible actions such as abstaining from idols, while helpful, are merely temporary fixes that will never bring true victory. Therefore, if we genuinely desire to experience life-changing freedom from temptation and sin, we must reconcile in our hearts and minds whether we trust the power of Scripture wholeheartedly. Keep in mind, God spoke creation into existence by the power of His spoken Word. Why then would we doubt His inspired, written Word as insufficient in any way?

"How can a young man keep his way pure? By guarding it according to your word. With my whole heart I seek you; let me not wander from your commandments! I have stored up your word in my heart, that I might not sin against you. Blessed are you, O LORD; teach me your statutes!"

— Psalm 119:9–12

While it might seem too good to be true, Scripture empowers us to destroy every stronghold the enemy uses to bind our hearts and enslave our minds. Therefore, we must trust that God's promises are capable of meeting our needs in every situation. When Satan tempted Jesus after forty days in the wilderness (Matt. 4:1-11), the only thing which mattered was that our Lord and Savior trusted the wisdom of Scripture and knew how to use it. That is how Jesus withstood the enemy's attack and we are wise to learn from the way of escape He chose to survive temptation, so that we too might do the same when our hour of testing arrives.

"Now, if our Lord and Master selected this true Jerusalem blade of the Word of God, let us not hesitate for a moment but grasp and hold fast this one true weapon of the saints in all times. Cast away the wooden sword of carnal reasoning. Trust not in human eloquence but arm yourselves with the solemn declaration of God, who cannot lie, and you need not fear Satan and all his hosts. Jesus selected the best weapon. What was best for Him is best for you."

— Charles Spurgeon
"Infallibility: Where To Find It And How To Use It," December 20, 1874.

God's way of escape is not nearly as complicated as we make it out to be. When we pray for the Lord to give us wisdom and discernment to make right choices in life, we need not wait for a response because He has already answered! The Bible, God's life-giving truth, is accessible to us every day of our lives. All we must do is tap into this gift He sovereignly provided for us. Often-times, we sit idle and wait for an epiphany from heaven when the answers we need are directly in front of us. Therefore, we must humble ourselves and open our Bibles. God is waiting to reveal His wisdom to us, but we must meet Him half-way and begin reading His Word to hear His still, small voice.

"Jesus answered, 'It is written, "Man shall not live by bread alone, but by every word that comes from the mouth of God."'"

— Matthew 4:4

Application

1. Which temptations cause you the most anxiety? Why are you worried about them?

2. What is Satan's most effective strategy to tempt you to sin?

3. Which overarching temptation (ease, comfort, fulfillment, or pleasure) best categorizes your personal struggles? How so?

4. Have you ever considered that God's Word is your ultimate way of escape? Why or why not?

5. What plans or preparations can you make to guard your heart and mind from yielding to temptation?

6. How can accountability become one of the most effective tools you use to escape the snares of temptation?

7. What distracts you from reading the Bible daily and studying God's Word? What changes can you make for it to become your #1 priority?

Prayer

Lord, Your Word is a lamp to my feet and a light to my path, yet I continue to default into self-protection mode when the enemy tempts me to sin. Why do I continue to think I am strong enough to resist temptation? It is as if Your truth goes in one ear and out the other. I hate how much I yield to my flesh. I need more self-control in my life, but I must also shift my perspective altogether and begin utilizing the sword of the spirit which You graciously provide. Help me lean upon Your Spirit and stop fighting my battles all alone. You are my way of escape and I need to start trusting You far more often. Amen.

CHAPTER 15

Help! I Am Regretful
(I'm tired of being ashamed of my past.)

Knowledge is critical to navigating the trials of life, but what happens when the absolute truth of God's Word convicts our sinful behavior? Do we instinctively react based upon our limited knowledge, or respond with wisdom and discernment? Case in point, Adam and Eve found themselves in a precarious situation one day in the Garden of Eden. God told them to enjoy the fruit of every tree they desired but specifically warned them not to eat from just one, the tree of knowledge, lest they die.

"And the woman said to the serpent, 'We may eat of the fruit of the trees in the garden, but God said, "You shall not eat of the fruit of the tree that is in the midst of the garden, neither shall you touch it, lest you die."'"

— *Genesis 3:2–3*

However, when temptation came, they willingly disobeyed God's singular command with little persuasion. Why? Perhaps it was because they had never been lied to before and did not know how to respond; maybe they genuinely thought the serpent had their best interest in mind? Keep in mind, they were all living in the Garden together, so they likely had no reason to doubt since they assumed everything God made was good. How then could the serpent's advice not be considered trustworthy?

"But the serpent said to the woman, 'You will not surely die. For God knows that when you eat of it your eyes will be opened, and you will be like God, knowing good and evil.'"

— Genesis 3:4–5

Without much coercion, the serpent twisted God's Word with a partial lie and Eve easily took the bait, changing the course of human history forevermore. Her decision to yield to temptation and cause Adam to do the same reveals how powerful discontentment with God's sovereign provision can be to those who desire various levels of fulfillment. However, it is imperative that we consider what happened moments after they ate from the tree of knowledge to avoid making a similar choice and suffer unending guilt, shame, and regret as well.

"Then the eyes of both were opened, and they knew that they were naked. And they sewed fig leaves together and made themselves loincloths."

— Genesis 3:7

Genesis 3:7 begins by stating that upon eating the fruit, "the eyes of both were opened, and they knew that they were naked." Immediately, they experienced a physical reaction to a decision which seemed insignificant at the time but carried immeasurable consequences for all eternity. In that moment, sin was awakened with knowledge being the tool which convicted their conscience and inevitably separated them from God's presence. They knew they had chosen poorly but did not realize how bad it truly was.

It is sobering to recognize how even the simplest decisions can result in grave consequences. Hindsight is always 20/20 when we yield to temptation and sin, but we must resist categorizing our sins as worthy of punishment vs. excusable. For instance, we would probably equate a trivial lie as different from murder. However, in God's economy, both separate us from His presence and require equal atonement on judgment day. There is no hierarchy of sin or distinction where one sin is worthy of judgment while another is not. Consequences of actions surely differ but the eternal impact of sin is consistent no matter the severity.

"But each person is tempted when he is lured and enticed by his own desire. Then desire when it has conceived gives birth to sin, and sin when it is fully grown brings forth death."

— James 1:14–15

Adam and Eve's experience should remind us that when we come face to face with the reality of our sins, clouds of confusion dissipate almost immediately. We clearly see the wretchedness of our depravity. As previously mentioned, it can be defined as the moment of clarity when sin is exposed as fatal poison. In an instant, we realize that what we insatiably desire is nothing more than a mirage on the horizon, promising fulfillment which will never come to fruition. The question is how should we respond after our moment of clarity arises to ensure we do not make the same foolish decisions again?

"I acknowledged my sin to you, and I did not cover my iniquity; I said, 'I will confess my transgressions to the LORD,' and you forgave the iniquity of my sin."

— Psalm 32:5

The apostle Paul experienced a moment of clarity after being blinded on the Damascus road by none other than Jesus Himself. Paul persecuted the church and felt justified having followers of Christ imprisoned or killed. Nevertheless, Jesus intervened and afflicted Paul, putting an instant stop to his wickedness. Three days later, something like scales fell from Paul's eyes. For the first time, he saw how depraved and lost he was spiritually. He came face to face with the reality of his grievous sins against the Lord and it literally broke his spirit, changing the trajectory of his life forever to the glory of Jesus' name.

> *"So Ananias departed and entered the house. And laying his hands on him he said, 'Brother Saul, the Lord Jesus who appeared to you on the road by which you came has sent me so that you may regain your sight and be filled with the Holy Spirit.' And immediately something like scales fell from his eyes, and he regained his sight. Then he rose and was baptized; and taking food, he was strengthened."*

> *— Acts 9:17–19*

That is why knowledge is so powerful. When we have been enlightened by the truth of God's Word, our sins are magnified and we realize how wretched we have become, unworthy to stand before the Lord on judgment day. When the veil of temptation is lifted and we finally see our sin for how unfulfilling it is, no longer are we wondering if the grass is greener on the other side. We know it is not. Yet at that point, the damage has been done and there is no turning back. We must live with the consequences of our actions, whether we like it or not, and learn from them to avoid making the same poor decisions moving forward.

> *"St. Augustine teaches us that there is in each man a Serpent, an Eve, and an Adam. Our senses and natural propensities are the Serpent; the*

excitable desire is the Eve; and reason is the Adam. Our nature tempts us perpetually; criminal desire is often excited; but sin is not completed till reason consents."

— *Blaise Pascal*
"The Thoughts of Blaise Pascal," 1849.

We can be absolutely sure that Adam and Eve had no idea how such a simple choice could have catastrophic consequences eternally. That is the power of sin when we take the Lord's judgment for granted. We fail to appreciate what we have till it is taken away. Sin completely severs our fellowship with God to the point where only a blood sacrifice from a spotless lamb (Jesus) is holy and sufficient to atone for our wickedness and restore our relationship with God in heaven. Adam and Eve never could have imagined that one singular decision would be so disastrous, to the point where they were expelled from the Garden of Eden and cast out in the darkness to survive on their own.

However, God did not abandon them completely. He loved them and continued to remain in fellowship despite their strained relationship because of sin. God's hand of protection was lifted as they chose for themselves which path they would take in life, but His love never ceased despite their sin. Blood sacrifices of animals were required to cleanse them from unrighteousness and atone for future sins, but God did not walk away. Life outside the Garden of Eden took on a different dimension compared to life within God's sovereign protection. However, temptation entered their relationship and drove a wedge between them and God, and we are the beneficiaries of their catastrophic decision.

"For if the blood of goats and bulls, and the sprinkling of defiled persons with the ashes of a heifer, sanctify for the purification of the flesh, how much more will the blood of Christ, who through the eternal Spirit offered

himself without blemish to God, purify our conscience from dead works to serve the living God."

— Hebrews 9:13–14

Once their eyes were opened, Genesis 3:7 goes on to say, "They knew that they were naked." For the first time, they recognized how bare they were before God—not merely in a physical sense but emotionally and spiritually as well. They understood what sin felt like in that moment. Guilt, shame, and regret poured over their hearts and minds as they considered the gravity of their decision to eat the forbidden fruit. Unfortunately, their first inclination was not to confess their sin nor seek reconciliation with God. Instead, they chose to instinctively cover up their decision by hiding from accountability.

"And they heard the sound of the LORD God walking in the garden in the cool of the day, and the man and his wife hid themselves from the presence of the LORD God among the trees of the garden."

— Genesis 3:8

Keep in mind, when we sin, we are typically not intoxicated by the idol itself but the presumed benefit it provides to our flesh. That is why temptation appeals to our physical senses (sight, smell, hearing, touch, and taste). Often, we are searching for something to make us feel better, dull the pain, help us forget, or discover new pleasure. That is why temptation is meant to lure us into thinking "X" is the solution to our problems—what we are ultimately missing from our lives to feel satisfied and complete. However, the pleasures of this world will not solve anything but only enslave us further if all our attention is focused on satisfying our fleshly desires no matter the cost.

Temptation only leads to further bondage because it cannot quench our thirst, no matter how many times we return to the well of idolatry and drink of its deadly poison. That is why sin is more equivalent to developing cancer than suffering a massive heart attack. Both can kill if left untreated, but cancer spreads quietly and discreetly in the shadows of our hearts over time and poisons our minds into thinking the pleasures of this world will eventually satisfy our desires. That is why we must reconcile our sins before they morph out of control and destroy everything and everyone in our path.

"We know that our old self was crucified with him in order that the body of sin might be brought to nothing, so that we would no longer be enslaved to sin. For one who has died has been set free from sin."

— *Romans 6:6–7*

The final piece of the puzzle came together when Adam and Eve "sewed fig leaves together and made themselves loincloths." Rather than confess their sin, they chose to cover up only to reap the consequences of their actions. What we often fail to realize from Genesis 3:7 is that Adam and Eve still had a choice to make after eating from the tree of knowledge. They could have owned their poor decisions, taken initiative, and confessed before God confronted them. However, they chose to hide in a failed attempt to cover up their sins and avoid taking full responsibility for their foolish actions.

"Where shall I go from your Spirit? Or where shall I flee from your presence? If I ascend to heaven, you are there! If I make my bed in Sheol, you are there!"

— *Psalm 139:7–8*

Keep in mind, there is a chasm which exists between saying, "I'm sorry!" and asking, "Would you please forgive me?" Those of us who have been caught sinning typically use "I'm sorry!" as a halfhearted attempt to minimize the consequences of our actions. However, taking initiative to confess sins and ask those we have sinned against to please forgive us can be the difference between reconciliation and bitterness or resentment. None of us are perfect, though. We all make poor choices from time to time. Thus, the difference between spiritual maturity and immaturity hinges upon whether we respond with wisdom and discernment before we get caught or react after the fact by attempting to minimize, downplay, or blame shift our sins.

We are no different than Adam and Eve. We run and hide all the time rather than accept full responsibility for our actions. However, if we want to learn from our decisions and sin no more, we cannot wait until we get caught to begin the process of reconciliation. We must lay down our pride, take the initiative, and confess our sins before it is too late. That is much easier said than done, but our spiritual maturity (or lack thereof) is on full display when we confront our sins head on. Therefore, initiative is key to repentance. It does not make up for the sins we have committed but conveys to those we have sinned against that our recognition, conviction, and remorse are honest, sincere, and Biblically repentant.

> *"But when he came to himself, he said, 'How many of my father's hired servants have more than enough bread, but I perish here with hunger! I will arise and go to my father, and I will say to him, "Father, I have sinned against heaven and before you. I am no longer worthy to be called your son. Treat me as one of your hired servants."'"*
>
> — *Luke 15:17–19*

Adam and Eve's decision may seem trivial compared to more egregious sins we struggle with daily, but their desire for equality with God set off a chain reaction which has plagued humanity ever since. The real question is how we will respond the next time we sin. Will we own our choices or shift into damage control mode? Will we humble ourselves and confess our sins, or hide in the shadows and further perpetuate greater idolatrous addictions? Will we return to God in repentance or continue to wander aimlessly in the wilderness alone? The Lord wants to free us from the shackles of guilt, shame, and regret, but we must lay down our pride at the foot of the cross and embrace repentance. Otherwise, we will reap what we sow and face eternal judgment for disobeying the Lord and His Word.

"And the LORD God commanded the man, saying, 'You may surely eat of every tree of the garden, but of the tree of the knowledge of good and evil you shall not eat, for in the day that you eat of it you shall surely die.'"

— Genesis 2:16–17

The choice is ultimately ours to make. However, let us never forget that our decisions <u>after</u> we yield to temptation are just as crucial as the decisions we make <u>before</u> we sin. We must also take spiritual leadership in our homes and ensure we are holding ourselves accountable, first and foremost, before our children. Setting a zero-tolerance standard by accepting full responsibility for the sins we commit is critical, both directly (like Eve when she took hold of the fruit and ate) and indirectly (like Adam when he failed to protect his wife). Accountability begins with taking the lead and humbling ourselves through godly grief so we are not held captive by guilt, shame, and regret but set free through repentance by the power of Jesus' name.

Application

1. Which sins in your life do you regret most? Why?
2. How have you categorized your sin's severity to minimize or avoid punishment?
3. Give an example of a simple choice you made which resulted in grave consequences. What did you learn?
4. If God has never abandoned you despite your sins, why do you remain in bondage to chains of regret?
5. How have you fallen victim to coveting God's knowledge and power? How has that led you to sin against the Lord?
6. What are your key takeaways from Adam and Eve's reactions (before and after they sinned) from which you can learn?
7. Why are godly grief and repentance key to overcoming regret?

Prayer

Lord, it is humbling to reflect upon the story of Adam and Eve and see how easily they fell to temptation and hid from the consequences of their actions. Unfortunately, I am no different because I regret many foolish decisions I have made throughout my life. I could have avoided pitfalls had I simply chosen to obey Your Word rather than satisfy my fleshly desires. Hindsight is 20/20, though, and I understand that my past has made me who I am today. Even though I took the long road to righteousness, I appreciate the journey You led me on to break me from my sins. Your glory is revealed in my weakness, and I would not be where I am today without Your loving discipline which drew me home to Your loving arms. Thank You, Lord, for saving me. Amen.

CHAPTER 16

Lord, Give Me Salvation
(Rescue me from pride and self-destruction.)

If there is one question every man, woman, and child must reconcile before judgment day it is simply, "What must I do to be saved?" Salvation is the most crucial decision of free will God cares about concerning humanity. However, there is general confusion (even in the church) regarding salvation among many believers and denominations. Thankfully, Ephesians 2:8-9 clearly articulates how a person must be saved to enter the kingdom of heaven. It also provides clarity regarding the reason good works play no part in salvation, other than testifying to a changed heart sold out for Christ.

"For by grace you have been saved through faith. And this is not your own doing; it is the gift of God, not a result of works, so that no one may boast."

— Ephesians 2:8–9

The challenge is that many people place themselves in the salvation equation and assume their good deeds influence God's favor. However, good works are nothing more than a by-product of salvation from a born-again, repentant heart. Works are not what saves a man, for no one other than God knows whether a person is truly saved. Therefore, it is not our responsibility to judge the eternal destination of others. Rather, we are better served owning our sins, seeking restitution, and ensuring our personal actions, first and foremost, reflect the transformation of a redeemed soul completely sold out to Christ and His Word.

"But be doers of the word, and not hearers only, deceiving yourselves. For if anyone is a hearer of the word and not a doer, he is like a man who looks intently at his natural face in a mirror. For he looks at himself and goes away and at once forgets what he was like."

— James 1:22–24

We have been saved by grace through faith, but what does that mean? Grace is simply unmerited favor. We cannot earn it, for it is freely given with no strings attached nor payment needed. Grace is often referred to as a gift because it is out of our control and completely at the discretion of the giver. From Scripture's perspective, grace is an extension of God's love because His righteous law demands that sin be atoned for. Therefore, grace is required to save us from God's imminent wrath and secure our eternity in heaven rather than hell.

"For the wrath of God is revealed from heaven against all ungodliness and unrighteousness of men, who by their unrighteousness suppress the truth. For what can be known about God is plain to them because God has shown it to them. For his invisible attributes, namely, his eternal power and divine nature, have been clearly perceived, ever since the creation of the world, in things that have been made. So they are without excuse."

— Romans 1:18–20

Keep in mind, saving grace is a limited time offer that requires acceptance of its validity and all-sufficiency. It is grounded by faith in the truth of God's Word, for one day we will die and God's sovereign grace will only benefit us if we have accepted His free gift of salvation before judgment day arrives. Waiting or prolonging a faith decision in Christ is simply naïve and foolish. None of us are guaranteed tomorrow and we cannot predict with certainty whether we will live to see another day. As a result, we must reconcile whether we believe what God's Word says about salvation through faith in Jesus Christ for the forgiveness of sins and make that decision today.

"For what is the hope of the godless when God cuts him off, when God takes away his life?"

— Job 27:8

Just because we have uttered a "prayer of salvation" does not necessarily mean we are truly saved as the Bible teaches. There must be a harvest of fruit in our lives which testifies to a transformed heart that has turned away from sin and toward God's standard of righteousness. We must not only believe God's Word is true cover-to-cover (which supports the validity of our faith decision) but accept His gift of salvation by grace through faith. We must live obediently to the authority of Scripture so that good works testify to our faith conversion rather than contradict it. In other words, faith in Christ requires that we count the cost and understand the Gospel message. For Scripture is the means by which we learn what that sacrifice entails, and why it ultimately matters in the grand scheme of eternity.

"Working together with him, then, we appeal to you not to receive the grace of God in vain. For he says, 'In a favorable time I listened to you,

and in a day of salvation I have helped you.' Behold, now is the favorable time; behold, now is the day of salvation."

— *2 Corinthians 6:1–2*

Let us be clear. Good works do not save us in any way. They merely pour out from a thankful heart, bathed in humility for the forgiveness of sins. However, some Christians believe works are a part of the salvation equation, which completely contradicts Ephesians 2:9 and confuses Christ-followers with false doctrine. Regardless of faith, they still believe their good works must outweigh the bad before they die, but they miss the point. Works testify to the work of the Holy Spirit in our hearts after we have come to salvation in Christ, for Jesus' blood is the only thing that matters because He died in our place.

Works are merely pay-it-forward opportunities whereby we extend love, grace, and mercy to others because God has likewise infinitely blessed us. They do not supplant or minimize the sacrifice Jesus made on the cross. Rather, they point others to Him as the true source of salvation. Good works are an opportunity to share the Gospel with others because they convey that we are no longer living for ourselves but Christ alone, for we are purchased by His blood. Therefore, good works are our tools for evangelism so we can testify to what Christ has done for the sins of humanity.

"You are the light of the world. A city set on a hill cannot be hidden. Nor do people light a lamp and put it under a basket, but on a stand, and it gives light to all in the house. In the same way, let your light shine before others, so that they may see your good works and give glory to your Father who is in heaven."

— *Matthew 5:14–16*

Our good works should testify that we are image bearers of Jesus Christ, reflecting His love to a lost world devoid of hope and salvation. They should never glorify ourselves but always point others to God who is the founder and perfecter of our faith (Heb. 12:2). In the same light, we must guard against leading others astray. For if we are living to glorify ourselves, whether we realize it or not, we diminish the eternal sacrifice Jesus made and present a false Gospel for others to mistakenly believe, trust, and follow.

"Therefore let us not pass judgment on one another any longer, but rather decide never to put a stumbling block or hindrance in the way of a brother."

— Romans 14:13

That is how false teachings such as "saved by grace, kept alive by works" have become stumbling blocks within the Christian church. For centuries, false teaching has been used to manipulate people through guilt, shame, and regret, promising assurance on the basis of their behavior. Countless Christians have been misled to believe their works have the ability to sway the Lord's grace and mercy. However, that is the essence of conditional love which is not Biblically supported in any way.

On the contrary, works testify to the power of saving grace working in our hearts and through our actions for the glory of God alone. There is nothing I can do to earn the Lord's favor. He loves me despite my wretchedness. If I believe His mind can be swayed by good works, though, then His grace is no longer sufficient. In essence, I am saying the blood of Jesus is not enough because I have to do my part to earn His favor and keep my salvation retroactive. Otherwise, I run the risk of losing my salvation, which is not supported by Scripture whatsoever.

"What good is it, my brothers, if someone says he has faith but does not have works? Can that faith save him? If a brother or sister is poorly clothed and lacking in daily food, and one of you says to them, 'Go in peace, be warmed and filled,' without giving them the things needed for the body, what good is that? So also faith by itself, if it does not have works, is dead."

— *James 2:14–17*

Countless people have passed away believing their good works could save them on judgment day, yet nothing could be further from the truth. Rather than accept Christ's gift of salvation as promised in Scripture by grace through faith alone, they chose to hedge their bet on a majority percentage of good works, assuming they could tip the morality scale in their favor to gain entrance into heaven. The only problem is the more we insert ourselves into the salvation equation, the more we diminish Jesus' sacrifice on the cross.

Unfortunately, those who rely on good works to save them are languishing in hell today with inconsolable regret because they assumed they could somehow earn God's favor and share in the glory of their salvation. Pride hindered them from relinquishing full control of their lives to God because they felt a need to earn their way to heaven rather than receive it. As a result, their eternal fate was sealed the moment they chose to disbelieve God's Word and reject the power of divine grace through faith alone in Jesus Christ as all-sufficient to save them.

"For there is no distinction: for all have sinned and fall short of the glory of God, and are justified by his grace as a gift, through the redemption that is in Christ Jesus, whom God put forward as a propitiation by his blood, to be received by faith."

— Romans 3:22–25

Many unbelievers struggle reconciling God's final judgment because they believe if He is loving, all people should be allowed in heaven when they die, regardless of their past. From their perspective, it seems unreasonable for a loving God to sentence people to eternity in hell. However, His holy law demands sin be atoned for, and those same naysayers reject the need to reconcile their sins and accept personal responsibility for their actions. That is why John 3:16-18 is such an encouragement because it explains not only how we can be saved, but why God chose to sacrifice His Son to save us from sin and death.

"For God so loved the world, that he gave his only Son, that whoever believes in him should not perish but have eternal life. For God did not send his Son into the world to condemn the world, but in order that the world might be saved through him. Whoever believes in him is not condemned, but whoever does not believe is condemned already, because he has not believed in the name of the only Son of God."

— John 3:16–18

Truly, salvation by grace through faith alone seems too good to be true. In our flesh, we feel the need to do something in return to earn our reward and pay back our debt, but that logic runs contrary to what Scripture teaches. Salvation is a free gift and we have no expectation by God other than to accept His eternal way of escape if we desire to evade our fate as sinners on judgment day. The Lord will not force our hand. He gives us a free-will choice. Therefore, we must relinquish our pride and believe His plan of salvation to spend eternity in heaven rather than hell. For we cannot save ourselves in any way, no matter how hard we try to do good works to earn our way to heaven.

As Jonathan Edwards once preached, what we deserve as "sinners in the hands of an angry God" is death. Granted, we can argue otherwise and attempt to minimize our sins to justify our actions. However, even if we have committed only one sin in our lifetime, we are still guilty of breaking God's law and subject to eternity in hell if we do not reconcile Ephesians 2:8-9 in our hearts before we die. It is as simple as that but also requires that we relinquish our pride, humble ourselves, and repent of our sins.

"For whoever keeps the whole law but fails in one point has become guilty of all of it."

— James 2:10

"For all who rely on works of the law are under a curse; for it is written, 'Cursed be everyone who does not abide by all things written in the Book of the Law and do them.' Now it is evident that no one is justified before God by the law, for 'The righteous shall live by faith.' But the law is not of faith, rather 'The one who does them shall live by them.'"

— Galatians 3:10–12

Ephesians 2:8-9 is not meant as a scare tactic to force a salvation decision, but rather a key to answering the most important question every man, woman, and child must reconcile in their hearts before they die. Regardless, some people will refuse to believe in a God who would sentence anyone to eternity in hell. However, what they fail to realize is how patient and forgiving He is and to provide a way of escape from eternal damnation through the blood of His Son whom He sacrificed for us.

All we must do is repent of our sins and accept God's grace through faith in Christ as our eternal substitute on judgment day. God did not save us because we loved Him but because He first loved us and prepared a way to reconcile our hearts back to Him. He did not have to save us but chose to because His love is endless. He gave us ample opportunity to reconcile our hearts to Him before judgment day and we are wise to accept His gift.

"He is the propitiation for our sins, and not for ours only but also for the sins of the whole world. And by this we know that we have come to know him, if we keep his commandments."

— *1 John 2:2–3*

"In this is love, not that we have loved God but that he loved us and sent his Son to be the propitiation for our sins."

— *1 John 4:10*

"All this is from God, who through Christ reconciled us to himself and gave us the ministry of reconciliation; that is, in Christ God was reconciling the world to himself, not counting their trespasses against them, and entrusting to us the message of reconciliation."

— *2 Corinthians 5:18–19*

Bottom-line, we must all accept the Father's unending grace through faith in Jesus Christ, making Him Lord and Savior of our lives forevermore. Grace does not wait for us to come home but meets us right where we are, healing our broken hearts, and reconciling our souls for eternity to the glory of Jesus' name. God knew we could not save ourselves, so He provided a better way. The question is whether we will surrender our pride and accept His free gift of salvation or roll the dice under the assumption that heaven is a free pass for everyone. The choice is ours, but we must choose wisely because tomorrow is not guaranteed and our time is eventually running out.

Application

1. What comes to mind when you think about salvation? What are you trying to escape from most?
2. Why is life after death the only type of salvation you should be concerned about?
3. If you are born-again and saved by grace through faith in Jesus, what else could possibly harm you? How so?
4. How do faith and works go hand-in-hand? What role do they play in the salvation debate?
5. Is salvation truly a free gift? Why or why not?
6. How has the enemy baited you into believing you can lose your salvation?
7. How have you mourned the loss of loved ones who rejected salvation by faith alone through grace in Christ?

Prayer

Lord, salvation is an emotional topic for me to reflect upon. I am eternally grateful for Your gift of salvation which forgives my sins. However, I am saddened by the reality that some people I know and love will not be present when I reach heaven one day. I know that eternal salvation is all that truly matters, yet I allow worldly fears to plague my mind and doubt whether I am saved. If only I would embrace that nothing could separate me from the love of Jesus, perhaps doubt and worry would no longer be a struggle. Help me trust that my eternal fate is sealed forevermore because my debt has been paid. I am set free by Your shed blood, Lord. Thank You for giving me far more than I deserve. Amen.

CHAPTER 17

Help! I Am Undisciplined

(I'm tired of lacking spiritual discipline.)

Boxing is a brutal and polarizing sport. People either love it or hate it. However, when viewed through a spiritual lens, boxing can help us better understand our faith and prepare our hearts and minds for the journey ahead. Boxing is all about commitment, determination, consistency, and work ethic. No man confidently steps into the ring without rigorously training his body to withstand the pain and suffering his opponent wishes to inflict upon him to win. To think otherwise would be complete foolishness! Why then do we assume we can subdue our spiritual enemy without similarly training our minds and planning our strategies of attack and defense?

"Do you not know that in a race all the runners run, but only one receives the prize? So run that you may obtain it. Every athlete exercises self-control in all things. They do it to receive a perishable wreath, but we an imperishable. So I do not run aimlessly; I do not box as one beating the air. But I discipline my body and keep it under control, lest after preaching to others I myself should be disqualified."

— 1 Corinthians 9:24–27

"Therefore, let anyone who thinks that he stands take heed lest he fall."

— 1 Corinthians 10:12

The challenge is there is a distinct difference between training for combat and being able to withstand the enemy's onslaught. We can discipline our minds and train our bodies to the best of our abilities, but if we let down our guard and assume we are well-protected without shoring up our weaknesses and addressing our insecurities, we will likely be headed for defeat. There is simply no training in the world which could prove sufficient for survival if we drop our hands, lower our defense, become stagnant in our posture, and allow the enemy to take a clean shot at us.

Keep in mind, the enemy will always look to exploit the cracks in our armor and widen those gaps in whatever way possible to expose our weaknesses. Granted, he already knows what they are, but often we have no clue where we are most vulnerable because we have allowed pride to distract our attention and cloud our judgment. Therefore, acting as if we can hide our insecurities from his knowledge is foolish. We are better served working tirelessly to shore up our defense and cover our blindside to not be easily exposed to attack moving forward.

"In your struggle against sin you have not yet resisted to the point of shedding your blood."

— Hebrews 12:4

What the enemy is more focused on is wearing down what we assume are our greatest strengths. He knows that if he can destroy our foundation of pride, all we have worked hard to accomplish will come crashing down upon our fragile psyche. That is why many people succumb to hopelessness in spiritual warfare because they focus too much on fixing their weaknesses without guarding their strengths as well.

"And he told them a parable, saying, 'The land of a rich man produced plentifully, and he thought to himself, "What shall I do, for I have nowhere to store my crops?" And he said, "I will do this: I will tear down my barns and build larger ones, and there I will store all my grain and my goods. And I will say to my soul, 'Soul, you have ample goods laid up for many years; relax, eat, drink, be merry.'" But God said to him, "Fool! This night your soul is required of you, and the things you have prepared, whose will they be?"'"

— Luke 12:16–20

Assumptions are the reason most of us struggle in our faith journey. We think we are further along in our spiritual maturity than we truly are and allow laziness to creep into our spiritual disciplines. Before we know it, our guard is down and heart exposed for the enemy to exploit and conquer. That is why most boxers deliver repeated body blows to weaken the core stamina of their opponent. Keep in mind, no trained boxer gets knocked down by a single punch to the abdomen, but consistent onslaught to a man's core will wear down his energy and present a strategic opportunity for a potential knockout punch.

The same concept applies spiritually. There is an infinite amount of credible demands on our lives which exasperate our minds and draw us away from quality time with God. Therefore, it should come as no surprise when trials overwhelm our hearts and drive us into a state of depression. The enemy knows that when busyness overwhelms our psyche, quality time in spiritual disciplines wanes, pulling us away from God's protection. Satan has all the time in the world to sit and wait patiently for us to let down our guard, so it should not surprise us when his repeated body blows finally knock us down for the count.

Examining how prepared we are for battle is critical too. If we desire to endure seasons of trial, we must take inventory of what knowledge and skills we have at our disposal rather than take them for granted. Keep in mind, a boxer is merely setting himself up for failure if he is only training his body and avoiding the psychological preparation he must master as well. Mental stamina is key to surviving constant attack, which in the spiritual realm means daily discipline abiding in Scripture for discernment and wisdom and communicating with God in prayer.

We are wise to comprehend how valuable Scripture is to every man determined to live for God's glory and not his own. That is why Paul emphatically warns us in 1 Corinthians 10:12 to recognize if we are leaning more on facts than assumptions. For when the enemy attempts to overwhelm our minds, we must be well prepared with facts to stand our ground and inevitably launch a counter-offensive. Guarding our flank from assumptions is key. It requires that we scrutinize our foundation of truth and examine what we genuinely believe.

"Be watchful, stand firm in the faith, act like men, be strong."

— 1 Corinthians 16:13

Undoubtedly, any man who does not train his mind will never last twelve rounds with his opponent. He will not last one round, all things considered. Once the first punch from his opponent connects, his mind will begin to shift into self-protection mode rather than offensive attack. That is why it is critical to recognize that we are always in the middle of a spiritual marathon, not a sprint. Our greatest asset is endurance, not strength, because victory comes to those who can discipline themselves and train for the long haul, come what may.

"Therefore, since we are surrounded by so great a cloud of witnesses, let us also lay aside every weight, and sin which clings so closely, and let us run with endurance the race that is set before us, looking to Jesus, the founder and perfecter of our faith, who for the joy that was set before him endured the cross, despising the shame, and is seated at the right hand of the throne of God."

— Hebrews 12:1–2

Oftentimes, we enter the ring of spiritual warfare intent on knocking Satan out with one single punch, because we are not necessarily prepared for a twelve-round battle. We assume that we are in fairly decent shape to hold our own, so we roll the dice and start swinging with all our might once we hear the bell ring. The problem is that our enemy is smarter than us and a true expert in the "rope-a-dope" technique. Therefore, he simply leans back against the ropes and allows us to swing relentlessly because he knows our punches are virtually ineffective to inflict any harm upon him.

Satan's strategy is all about wearing us down. Because when we are tired, we will lower our defense and allow him ample opportunity to exploit our weaknesses and knock us out in return. That is why pride is our greatest adversary. In many ways, it baits us into assuming we are stronger and more equipped than we truly are. Pride says, "I got this!" However, it is also the primary reason we find ourselves lying down on the ring canvas battered, bruised, helpless, and defeated.

"For everyone who exalts himself will be humbled, and he who humbles himself will be exalted."

— Luke 14:11

If only we would stick to our Biblical training, we would stand a far better chance of remaining upright in our faith than knocked down repeatedly. Keep in mind, boxers lean heavily on maintaining a consistent rhythm with their movement. They want to keep their guard up, breathing in check, punch sequence smooth, and footwork balanced to work off muscle memory than momentary thought. That is why consistent training and self-control are critical to long-term success.

The same goes for spiritual disciplines. Keeping a frequent and consistent rhythm in Bible study and prayer is paramount, but knowledge will only get us so far if we are not applying what we are learning. We must practice what we preach and not fall victim to living hypocritically. Truly, endurance comes when we invest our blood, sweat, and tears by allowing the Spirit to refine our character through constant communication with God in prayer. Only then will we tune out the noise of the world which distracts us from hearing what the Lord has to say to our hearts.

Pain comes with building spiritual endurance because persecution is real for those who live unashamed of the Gospel. How then should we respond in faith? Truly, what separates a good boxer from a great one comes down to how trained and prepared he is to take a punch, not deliver one. Any man can walk into the ring and begin throwing haymakers until exhaustion takes over, but what happens when his opponent strikes back and knocks him to the canvas?

Oftentimes, the enemy will knock us down and bait us into believing all hope is lost, so why get back up again? Why endure pain and suffering if we do not have to? Satan held the same posture and whispered identical lies when Jesus accepted defeat at Calvary and died on the cross for our sins. However, what the enemy did not anticipate was that on the third day, Christ would rise from the grave and defeat death once and for all.

"Now I would remind you, brothers, of the gospel I preached to you, which you received, in which you stand, and by which you are being saved, if you hold fast to the word I preached to you—unless you believed in vain. For I delivered to you as of first importance what I also received: that Christ died for our sins in accordance with the Scriptures, that he was buried, that he was raised on the third day in accordance with the Scriptures."

— 1 Corinthians 15:1–4

May we never forget that our Lord and Savior was down for the count but rose again! Therefore, despite how many times we get knocked down by pride, sin, and temptation, we can turn back to God in repentance and rise again to live another day. That is the beauty of the Gospel's redemptive message of salvation. Consequently, we should never feel defeated because Jesus is on our side and His victory over sin and death enables us to fight on no matter how defeated we may feel in the moment.

"For the righteous falls seven times and rises again, but the wicked stumble in times of calamity."

— Proverbs 24:16

Only the hopeless remain down for the count. However, we who are alive in Christ have victory in our grasp because of what Jesus did on the cross, not what we attempt to do in the hope of saving ourselves. Thus, we must embrace our born-again identity and learn from our poor decisions so we are well-equipped to go another twelve rounds with Satan until the Lord calls us home to eternity in heaven. That does not mean the road to victory will be easy. It simply means we appreciate the spiritual disciplines we learn far more when we sacrifice our time and work hard to attain them.

Application

1. Would you consider yourself spiritually undisciplined? Why or why not?

2. How can you better prepare to defend yourself spiritually? What tools do you have at your disposal to defend yourself?

3. What do you assume are your greatest strengths? How can they become your greatest weaknesses if you are not careful?

4. How has Satan used pride to sabotage your spiritual growth?

5. Which everyday distractions draw you away from quality time with God?

6. If your spiritual disciplines need more training, where will you turn for help? Why does it matter?

7. How can you preach the Gospel to yourself and be reminded that you have victory in Jesus forevermore?

Prayer

Lord, as much as I want to believe I am rock-solid in my faith journey, I am in desperate need of discipline. Busyness has overwhelmed my mind and plagued my schedule. I often find myself struggling to find time to pray or read my Bible. The danger is I am leaning far more on my own understanding when I should be running to You for wisdom and discernment. Help me train my mind better so that when spiritual warfare ensues, I am ready for battle. Help me protect my presumed strengths as well as my weaknesses so I am not self-deceived. I am nothing without You. Therefore, convict me in areas I need to improve upon and help me discipline my heart to avoid spiritual defeat. Amen.

CHAPTER 18

Lord, Give Me Wisdom

(Illuminate my mind with Your truth.)

How would one define "profitable?" Would we explain it in financial terms? Probably, because profitability is the net result of revenue minus expenses, or what is gained vs. invested. Do we ever think of profitability from a spiritual lens, though? We are encouraged to invest our time, energy, and resources to build greater spiritual disciplines in our lives. However, are we motivated out of burden or compulsion because we are expected to as Christians, or on the residual dividends we will earn on our strategic investments based on profitability gained?

"Then Jesus told his disciples, 'If anyone would come after me, let him deny himself and take up his cross and follow me. For whoever would save his life will lose it, but whoever loses his life for my sake will find it. For what will it profit a man if he gains the whole world and forfeits his soul? Or what shall a man give in return for his soul?'"

— Matthew 16:24–26

The key to success is looking at our faith journey as a long-term, spiritual investment with a guaranteed, not variable, rate of return. Granted, there are no drawbacks associated with giving our lives to Christ. He paid our ransom and secured our eternal freedom from the power of sin and death. The only risk we take is not accepting Jesus' gift of salvation for the forgiveness of sins and appreciating the wisdom He gives us through Scripture as outlined in Paul's second letter to Timothy.

> *"All Scripture is breathed out by God and profitable for teaching, for reproof, for correction, and for training in righteousness, that the man of God may be complete, equipped for every good work."*
>
> — *2 Timothy 3:16–17*

Just imagine walking into a bank and being told you could open a savings account with an annual percentage rate (APR) of 100%. You would immediately invest every penny you could spare because your financial investment would be doubled based on a highly profitable interest rate. The same principle applies spiritually, except that God's APR is not less than 0.50% like most banks, but infinity! It is even greater than winning a mega lottery because what we profit far exceeds monetary value. It is a priceless gift, free of charge, which should be considered with the utmost reverence and respect for God we can muster.

How then do we guarantee yielding a profit? It all begins with examining what we invest into our spiritual development so we might gain perspective regarding the blessings God bestows on those who apply His Word. It all comes down to risk assessment, investment, and profit. Therefore, we must consider the following examples which help clarify potential blessings that come to those who obey Scripture's teachings unconditionally and without hesitation. For blessings will overflow to those who discipline themselves to seek after righteousness, and we are wise to follow that guaranteed formula for success.

Examples

- If I seek wisdom and discernment from God's Word (investment), I gain understanding (profit).

- If I repent of my sins to God and others (investment), I gain forgiveness and reconciliation (profit).

- If I make a public profession of faith in Jesus Christ (investment), I gain salvation (profit).

- If I learn from my mistakes and change my wicked ways (investment), I gain wisdom (profit).

- If I love my wife as Christ loved the church (investment), I gain the fruit of the Spirit (profit).

- If I keep no secrets from my loved ones (investment), I gain trust and respect (profit).

- If I share my personal struggles and failures with my family (investment), I gain prayer and accountability (profit).

- If I live with moral integrity (investment), I gain credibility with others (profit).

- If I resist temptations to sin (investment), I gain contentment and peace of mind (profit).

No matter how we slice it, we gain far more than we realize when we discipline ourselves to invest time reading God's Word, for the Lord blesses and honors those who prioritize Him first in their lives. Jesus did not force His message of salvation upon anyone. He simply gave us a choice to either continue following the pattern of this world or turn our hearts back to Him and accept His gift of grace, mercy, and forgiveness. Keep in mind, there are no strings attached or fine print hidden in the salvation contract Jesus signed. His blood merely purchased our eternal freedom.

2 Timothy 3:16-17 becomes profitable when we discipline our minds to accept and receive God's absolute truth with teachable hearts. The key is we must be patient, humble, and welcome accountability, for no man who stands before Almighty God with pride in his heart will receive the gift of righteousness the Lord has in store. Rather, he will merely store up wrath for himself on judgment day because of his unwillingness to lay down his pride at the foot of the cross.

"Everyone who is arrogant in heart is an abomination to the LORD; be assured, he will not go unpunished."

— Proverbs 16:5

Many self-proclaimed Christians find themselves face to face with the paradox of reconciling their past and present identities. They fail to realize that their continued struggles are more a result of trying to put a square peg (old self) in a round hole (new self) than anything else. When we place faith in Jesus Christ for the forgiveness of sins and accept His free gift of salvation, we are no longer held captive by our past. We have been redeemed and our sins are washed away. We have abundant life and, therefore, a new identity in Christ.

"Or do you not know that the unrighteous will not inherit the kingdom of God? Do not be deceived: neither the sexually immoral, nor idolaters, nor adulterers, nor men who practice homosexuality, nor thieves, nor the greedy, nor drunkards, nor revilers, nor swindlers will inherit the kingdom of God. And such were some of you. But you were washed, you were sanctified, you were justified in the name of the Lord Jesus Christ and by the Spirit of our God."

— 1 Corinthians 6:9–11

Why then would we return to the sins of our past which once enslaved us? Are we attempting to steer our ship without a compass to guide the way? Do we not realize we are hopelessly lost without Scripture to illuminate our path toward righteousness? Most Christians drift wayward in their faith only to be consumed by an ocean of relative truth when storms blow in from across the horizon. If only we would realize that God has equipped us with everything we need to survive, new life in Christ would not seem like such a struggle. However, the remedy to our problems is quite simple. Open our Bibles and begin reading, because God inspired its composition so we would not have to live another day without His knowledge and wisdom.

"How precious to me are your thoughts, O God! How vast is the sum of them! If I would count them, they are more than the sand."

— *Psalm 139:17–18*

Where the rubber meets the road is whether we genuinely believe God's Word is true. Paul wrote that all Scripture is breathed out by God, which means we each have a crucial decision to make whether we realize it or not. We must ask ourselves, "Do I believe the Bible is absolute truth, cover to cover, and will I embrace its holiness as righteous and pure, its inerrancy without fault, and its infallibility which never fails as my faith doctrine?" Outside of asking, "What must I do to be saved?" it is arguably the most pivotal and life-changing question we must reconcile, sooner rather than later. For if we doubt or distrust even one verse of Scripture then, in theory, it cannot be trusted as absolute truth because we believe it can be refuted as false doctrine. Again, that is where many Christians falter because they are unwilling to endorse Scriptural truth cover to cover. They fail to understand how Jesus and the Bible are intertwined.

"If any of you lacks wisdom, let him ask God, who gives generously to all without reproach, and it will be given him. But let him ask in faith, with no doubting, for the one who doubts is like a wave of the sea that is driven and tossed by the wind."

— James 1:5–6

Whether Scripture is inerrant and infallible is an all or nothing decision we must reconcile. There is not a 99.99% option which allows us to choose what is true from the pages of Scripture. Faith and trust in the Bible are a package deal for those who claim to be followers of Christ. It is the foundation of our personal faith doctrine as believers because it clearly articulates our standard of morality to those around us. Anything less undermines our faith and calls into question what we believe altogether.

Assuming we affirm and believe the Bible is absolute truth, applying what it teaches and defending its position on morality becomes easier. No longer are we merely stating our opinion but endorsing what the Lord has to say. When our personal doctrine mirrors God's Word, we are removed from direct attack and persecution for our beliefs. Truly, we are not at war with society but culture, which directly opposes the Creator of the universe. That one truth is incredibly profound. It allows us to make judgment calls on sinful behavior without feeling personally attacked. For the Lord is our strength and shield, and He will protect those who stand unashamed of His Word.

"So everyone who acknowledges me before men, I also will acknowledge before my Father who is in heaven, but whoever denies me before men, I also will deny before my Father who is in heaven."

— Matthew 10:32–33

No matter our circumstances, we can rest assured in the sufficiency of Scripture to not only teach, reproof, and correct our personal behavior, but equip us for whatever trials lie ahead. No matter what the enemy throws our way, we are safe and secure to accomplish His will because God is ultimately in control, not us. Therefore, we should fear no evil because the Lord's rod and staff comfort us when we are persecuted for our faith. All we must do is remain steadfast in our beliefs and trust His Word without doubt or hesitation.

"No weapon that is fashioned against you shall succeed, and you shall refute every tongue that rises against you in judgment. This is the heritage of the servants of the LORD and their vindication from me, declares the LORD."

— Isaiah 54:17

Far too often, we cower in the face of adversity when we speak boldly to defend Scripture. Yet for whatever reason, when our culture screams louder in opposition against us, we believe the lie that our beliefs are devoid of power to destroy Satan's stronghold. However, if we would simply wield the sword of the Spirit (God's Word), we would quickly realize that nothing the enemy throws our way can prosper. At the name of Jesus, demons cower in fear! Therefore, let us trust in God's provision and not give the enemy a foothold to hold us captive. For Satan is powerless to defeat the Lord almighty, and he will ultimately be destroyed at the final judgment of this fallen world.

"For the LORD your God is he who goes with you to fight for you against your enemies, to give you the victory."

— Deuteronomy 20:4

Application

1. What makes a person wise or foolish in God's eyes?
2. Do you believe God is the true source of all wisdom? Why or why not?
3. How is it helpful to consider wisdom from an investment vs. profit perspective?
4. How different would your life be if you sought the Lord's wisdom, first and foremost, in every big decision you made?
5. What issues do you struggle with that you desperately need wisdom, discernment, and counsel?
6. Why does God want you to learn from the sins of your past? What impact does your personal experience have on wisdom?
7. Why must a Christian believe the Bible is 100% true, cover-to-cover? How does that impact your view of wisdom?

Prayer

Lord, as foolish as it seems, I must be reminded daily of how awesome You are. The perfect design of Your creation is evident all around me. Your power and majesty are undeniable. Yet when it comes to the decisions I make in life, both big and small, I lean more on my own understanding rather than Your Word for wisdom and clarity. Why am I so foolish? How can I be given the keys to the kingdom, per se, but choose to live in poverty? Your Word is life—priceless and without compare. Help me appreciate what a treasure I have before me when I open my Bible and begin reading Your absolute truth. I pray I never again take for granted the immeasurable gift of Your wisdom. Amen.

CHAPTER 19

Help! I Am Desperate
(I'm tired of feeling hopeless and discontent.)

When we have come to our wits end, we can rest assured that tomorrow is a new day for those who trust in the Lord Jesus Christ for salvation. No matter what difficulties we may be facing, the simple assurance that tomorrow is a fresh opportunity to begin anew is life-giving truth. The prospect of not being held captive by memories of the past can mean the difference between surviving seasons of trials and tribulations, or throwing in the towel and surrendering to fear, hopelessness, and despair.

> *"The steadfast love of the LORD never ceases; his mercies never come to an end; they are new every morning; great is your faithfulness. 'The LORD is my portion,' says my soul, 'therefore I will hope in him.' The LORD is good to those who wait for him, to the soul who seeks him. It is good that one should wait quietly for the salvation of the LORD."*
>
> — *Lamentations 3:22–26*

Oftentimes, we become so focused on the storms surrounding us that we lose sight of how temporary they truly are. Yes, we live in a fallen world. As such, life will bring incredible challenges and pain. However, that does not mean we have reason to accept final defeat. We choose whether we will react or respond to difficult life circumstances which determines how well we manage trials that inevitably come our way.

Regardless of the destructive and relentless waves which crash upon the foundation of our faith, as born-again followers of Jesus Christ, we know our joy will be permanently restored the day we embark upon eternity and see our Savior face to face. It does not matter what afflictions we endure now or in the future. For as the writer of Lamentations reminds us, tomorrow promises continual blessings to those who place eternal faith, hope, and trust in Jesus Christ as their personal Lord and Savior.

> *"I bless the LORD who gives me counsel; in the night also my heart instructs me. I have set the LORD always before me; because he is at my right hand, I shall not be shaken."*
>
> — *Psalm 16:7–8*

The key to finding lasting peace for our weary souls begins by remembering how faithful God has been. Spiritual markers are a practical way of preaching the Gospel to our hearts as a means of strengthening our foundation of faith. They are tangible life experiences from our past which remind us that God is active in our lives. They prove His faithfulness through moments in time where He performed powerful acts of love which could only be attributed to His sovereign grace and mercy.

> *"Then Joshua called the twelve men from the people of Israel, whom he had appointed, a man from each tribe. And Joshua said to them, 'Pass on before the ark of the LORD your God into the midst of the Jordan and take up each of you a stone upon his shoulder, according to the number of the tribes of the people of Israel, that this may be a sign among you.*

When your children ask in time to come, "What do those stones mean to you?" then you shall tell them that the waters of the Jordan were cut off before the ark of the covenant of the LORD. When it passed over the Jordan, the waters of the Jordan were cut off. So these stones shall be to the people of Israel a memorial forever.'"

— Joshua 4:4–7

When our spirits are tired and weary, we need reminders which bolster our faith—moments where God supernaturally steps into our circumstances and makes His presence known by rescuing us from our affliction. Granted, that does not mean we ignore the pain we are experiencing, but that we self-medicate with Scripture which connects absolute truth with personal experience. Jesus taught that worry cannot add time to our lives, yet we repeatedly yield to anxiety when there are examples all around which prove His faithfulness. Why then do we doubt He will meet our needs? Is He not capable of miraculously blessing us in ways we cannot explain?

"Therefore do not be anxious, saying, 'What shall we eat?' or 'What shall we drink?' or 'What shall we wear?' For the Gentiles seek after all these things, and your heavenly Father knows that you need them all. But seek first the kingdom of God and his righteousness, and all these things will be added to you."

— Matthew 6:31–33

What we learn in spiritual marker moments is that God gives tangible evidence of His grace at strategic points in our lives to prove that His promises are true. Scripture does not teach that personal experience must affirm absolute truth to be valid, but rather how God miraculously shows up in timely ways we can physically sense. He wants to remind us that He loves us and will always meet our greatest needs if we continue to trust Him.

Firsthand experiences embolden our faith in the validity of Scripture, whereas spiritual markers are a practical means of strengthening our resolve and guarding our minds from doubt, fear, worry, and anxiety. They affirm the centrality of the Gospel in our lives and testify to how gracious the Lord has been despite our difficult circumstances and seasons of life. They are not required to validate our faith, but they prove beneficial when our weary souls need to be reminded that God cares deeply about our spiritual well-being.

Preaching the Gospel to our hearts is a spiritual discipline of meditating on God's Word and washing our minds with the cleansing power of His infinite wisdom. Self-preaching reminds us of who we are in Christ and draws us into intimate fellowship with our Father in heaven. When we read, study, and reflect upon Scripture, our minds are trained to filter everything we see and hear through the lens of absolute truth. Therefore, we need not fear making wrong decisions in life because our discernment is based upon the wisdom of God rather than human logic.

"Riches do not profit in the day of wrath, but righteousness delivers from death."

— Proverbs 11:4

"For the word of God is living and active, sharper than any two-edged sword, piercing to the division of soul and of spirit, of joints and of marrow, and discerning the thoughts and intentions of the heart. And no creature is hidden from his sight, but all are naked and exposed to the eyes of him to whom we must give account."

— Hebrews 4:12–13

When we are tired and weary, our minds are prone to wander toward worldly wisdom. In turn, we begin to assume God's love, grace, mercy, and faithfulness are conditional. We begin to question our faith because our spiritual diet has shifted from feasting on absolute truth, which satisfies our needs, to relative truth which only leaves us parched and empty. It is an unfortunate position to find ourselves when we cannot recognize a counterfeit because we have not studied the original. However, far too many of us have a cloud of dust building on the covers of our Bibles because they have not been opened in a long time.

"Not everyone who says to me, 'Lord, Lord,' will enter the kingdom of heaven, but the one who does the will of my Father who is in heaven. On that day many will say to me, 'Lord, Lord, did we not prophesy in your name, and cast out demons in your name, and do many mighty works in your name?' And then will I declare to them, 'I never knew you; depart from me, you workers of lawlessness.'"

— Matthew 7:21–23

How then do we overcome our propensity toward self-reliance and guard our hearts against spiritual malnourishment? The answer lies in our ability to shift perspective and remind ourselves that the Bible is living and active, not merely historical. When temptation is at critical intensity and we are wrestling with yielding to sin, God's Word must transform from merely ink on a page to life-giving truth in our hearts and minds. Therefore, to guard our hearts from the relative wisdom of this world, we must feast upon the bounty of absolute truth God provides in His Word. For by preaching the Gospel to ourselves, we ensure that our minds are grounded in wisdom so we can overcome evil desires which wage war against the Holy Spirit who dwells within our hearts.

While spiritual markers and self-preaching help protect our hearts and minds in the moment, Scripture reminds us that the future is bright for those who place their hope and trust in the Lord, because His mercies are new every morning. It does not matter what calamities we may be facing today. Tomorrow is our chance to leave pain and heartache behind and refresh our souls with newfound hope. Therefore, we can clear our heads when the sun rises because we are no longer consumed by the past or present, which unapologetically reminds us of the trials we are facing and tempts us to despair all over again.

"Sing praises to the LORD, O you his saints, and give thanks to his holy name. For his anger is but for a moment, and his favor is for a lifetime. Weeping may tarry for the night, but joy comes in the morning."

— *Psalm 30:4–5*

In the moment, it is difficult to remember that we can push the restart button on our minds. Spiritual warfare can often be so intense that we struggle seeing past what is directly before us. Those who struggle with suicidal thoughts know this pattern well because tomorrow feels like a distant mirage that will never come to fruition. Their psyche is frozen in time and so consumed with unquenchable despair that they cannot fathom that rescue is even possible from a stronghold of hopelessness. Moreover, isolation takes over and tempts them to believe they are all alone in their suffering and misery.

I can recall specific points in my life when thoughts of suicide tempted my mind. The storms of life I faced in specific seasons made me question whether my loved ones would be better off without me. Darkness clouded my better judgment and I could not see past today and trust in the hope of tomorrow. The enemy had stolen my joy and I was held captive by despair until God intervened and saved me. His Word reminded me that I was not forgotten, abandoned, or alone, because I was His beloved child and my true identity was in Christ, not my pain and sorrow.

"In peace I will both lie down and sleep; for you alone, O LORD, make me dwell in safety."

— Psalm 4:8

It is important to recognize that God has engineered our bodies to require rest to recharge our emotional batteries and allow our minds to shut down for a period before they burn out. The more we deprioritize rest, the greater likelihood we will make critical mistakes because our decision-making ability is impaired. It is impossible to function for any considerable length of time without ensuring our bodies receive the sleep needed to survive. Why then would we assume our minds, which require emotional and psychological rest, be any different?

For many, we have been baited to assume the things of this world, which torment our minds and drive us into depression, will never fade. We assume hopelessness will be our companion forevermore and grow accustomed to tolerating pain rather than seeking a remedy. In turn, we refuse to let go and allow our minds to decompress because we have given up hope that tomorrow will be any different. However, if we would simply reject the lie we have bought into, we would realize that no matter what trials we may face, joy comes in the morning to those who trust in the Lord alone for salvation.

"Behold, the hour is coming, indeed it has come, when you will be scattered, each to his own home, and will leave me alone. Yet I am not alone, for the Father is with me. I have said these things to you, that in me you may have peace. In the world you will have tribulation. But take heart; I have

overcome the world."

— John 16:32–33

Just as Jesus rose from the grave, our hope in the joy of tomorrow is also resurrected because we know salvation comes to those who trust in His name. Therefore, why would we ever fear the memories of our past or the harsh reality of our present trials? If victory was provided once and for all when Christ defeated sin and death upon the cross of Calvary, there is no need to hide when the enemy attempts to steal our joy. Satan holds no sovereign power over us. Rather, we can rejoice in our sufferings because Jesus paid our debt and eternally set us free.

"I said of this poor body, 'You have not yet been newly created. The venom of the old serpent still taints you. But you shall yet be delivered. You shall rise again if you die and are buried, or you shall be changed if the Lord should suddenly come today. You, poor body, which drags me down to the dust in pain and sorrow, even you shall rise and be remade in the redemption of the body. For the new creation has begun in me, with God's down payment of his Spirit.' Oh beloved, can't you rejoice in this? I encourage you to do so. Rejoice in what God is doing in this new creation! Let your whole spirit be glad! Leap down, you waterfalls of joy! Overflow with gladness! Let loose the torrents of praise!"

— Charles Spurgeon
"God Rejoicing In The New Creation," July 5, 1891.

God intimately knows us. He knows the battles we face and how much we struggle believing that tomorrow is a fresh opportunity to overcome trials. However, we often doubt when we should believe and become anxious when we should trust Him. Why? If we are more precious to our Father in heaven than the birds of the air or the grass of the fields, why do we struggle finding rest for our tired and weary souls? Why do we doubt the Lord when He has proven faithful time and again despite our doubt of His sovereignty?

"Look at the birds of the air: they neither sow nor reap nor gather into barns, and yet your heavenly Father feeds them. Are you not of more value than they? And which of you by being anxious can add a single hour to his span of life?"

— Matthew 6:26–27

In many ways, it all comes back to the centrality of our faith and in whom we place our trust. If we rely upon ourselves, we are destined to succumb to fear, doubt, and worry, and ride a wave of emotions all the way to despair and hopelessness. But if our faith is in Christ, we are empowered by the absolute truth of God's Word to withstand the storms of life which seek to destroy us. Therefore, we are empowered to consider our trials as joy by remembering our spiritual markers, preaching the Gospel to our hearts, and resting in the blessed assurance of tomorrow's hope and promise of salvation.

"Therefore, brothers, since we have confidence to enter the holy places by the blood of Jesus, by the new and living way that he opened for us through the curtain, that is, through his flesh, and since we have a great priest over the house of God, let us draw near with a true heart in full assurance of faith, with our hearts sprinkled clean from an evil conscience and our bodies washed with pure water. Let us hold fast the confession of our hope without wavering, for he who promised is faithful."

— Hebrews 10:19–23

Application

1. Which trials, past and present, have left your heart, mind, and soul feeling desperate and hopeless?

2. Why is it critical to wash your mind with the absolute truth of Lamentations 3:22–26 when you are tired and weary?

3. Reflect upon the spiritual markers in your life. How has God revealed Himself to you in a supernatural way?

4. What does it mean to preach the Gospel to your heart daily? How can God's truth impact your attitude and temperament?

5. If the mercies of God are new every morning, why would you allow your mind to succumb to fear, doubt, and worry?

6. Why must you intentionally plan to rest? How is sleep critical for emotional, psychological, and spiritual well-being?

7. How can you count your trials as joy more often? Why does it matter?

Prayer

Lord, despite my best efforts, I am simply tired and desperate for the rest only You can provide. Help me abandon my feeble attempts to rescue myself when the walls are closing in on me. I have no power to overcome Satan without Your Spirit guiding me. I confess that I often fail to relinquish control to You when I am on the verge of breaking down physically, emotionally, psychologically, and spiritually. Your Word is light to my weary soul and I need to read it daily to have any shot at resisting the enemy's evil schemes. You are my rock and my salvation Lord. Help me to never doubt Your grace and mercy again. Amen.

CHAPTER 20

Lord, Give Me Deliverance

(Grant me victory to the glory of Your name.)

Being a Christian can be incredibly lonely, but following Jesus is worth it. Although this world is not our eternal home, we are called to live as salt and light to lost souls who are destined to spend eternity in hell if we do not speak truth in love and warn them of God's impending judgment. Evangelism is not easy, though. In many ways, it forces us out of our comfort zone into a hostile environment where persecution is real and the enemy is poised to attack us at any moment. That is why we must always be ready to defend Jesus and His Word and accept the inevitable consequences of living counter-culturally.

"Many are the afflictions of the righteous, but the LORD delivers him out of them all."

— Psalm 34:19

"Preach the word; be ready in season and out of season; reprove, rebuke, and exhort, with complete patience and teaching."

— 2 Timothy 4:2

Keep in mind, Psalm 34:19 challenges us to live counter to religion as well, speaking in sharp contrast against false doctrine such as the "prosperity gospel" (Word of Faith movement) which manipulates Jesus and holy Scripture for financial gain. No, the path of righteousness is narrow indeed, and those who choose to obey the Lord will undoubtedly endure affliction for their faith with no guarantee of riches this side of heaven. Truly, following Christ comes at a cost, and we must remember that truth daily.

"Enter by the narrow gate. For the gate is wide and the way is easy that leads to destruction, and those who enter by it are many. For the gate is narrow and the way is hard that leads to life, and those who find it are few."

— Matthew 7:13–14

Psalm 34:19 begins with a sobering reminder that living for righteousness' sake will require us to experience pain, distress, and heartache as part of our sanctification. Ironically, those are not marketing slogans churches use today to attract unbelievers to salvation. Scripture is clear that the path of righteousness is not based on how much wealth or prosperity we accumulate for ourselves, but how willing we are to sacrifice all if God calls us to forsake everything we hold dear to follow Him. How then will we respond when our number is called?

"Jesus said to him, 'If you would be perfect, go, sell what you possess and give to the poor, and you will have treasure in heaven; and come, follow me.' When the young man heard this he went away sorrowful, for he had great possessions."

— Matthew 19:21–22

Granted, sacrifice is never easy. At times, God assesses our loyalty of heart and allegiance to Him with trials designed to produce spiritual markers we can remember in the future. They testify to the power of the Holy Spirit who dwells in our hearts and gives us confidence to endure suffering and affliction for righteousness' sake. Spiritual markers also affirm God's faithfulness amid the storms of life and deepen our commitment to Him. They connect our lives to Jesus in a real and literal sense. For when we are mocked and ridiculed for defending what the Bible teaches, we are intimately united with Christ than ever before through the bond of persecution.

"Indeed, all who desire to live a godly life in Christ Jesus will be persecuted, while evil people and impostors will go on from bad to worse, deceiving and being deceived."

— 2 Timothy 3:12–13

"If the world hates you, know that it has hated me before it hated you. If you were of the world, the world would love you as its own; but because you are not of the world, but I chose you out of the world, therefore the world hates you."

— John 15:18–19

Countless martyrs have died with peace, joy, and contentment in their hearts because they tasted the bitterness of persecution for the Gospel of salvation. That does not mean persecution is required to experience God's presence more intimately, but that suffering for righteousness' sake is the mark of a true disciple of Jesus. It means we share in all phases of His death, burial, and resurrection when we die to ourselves and trust that our lives are better because of Him, not in spite of His name.

"All the afflictions of God's people are designed, under His gracious management – to test, to make manifest, and to exercise those graces and virtues which He has implanted in them. Though afflictions in themselves are not joyous but grievous, nevertheless they yield the peaceable fruits of righteousness in those who are exercised thereby. Afflictions serve to quicken the spirit of devotion in us; and to rouse us from that formality and indifference which frequently attend a long course of ease and prosperity. We are constrained to seek God with sincerity and fervor, when His chastening hand is upon us, since we then feel our absolute need of that help and deliverance, which He alone can give us."

— John Fawcett
"Christ Precious," 1799.

Righteousness is not a word commonly used in our culture today, yet the ESV Bible references it 264 times. Why then do we not talk more about it? From a human perspective, righteousness centers around purity of heart and striving for holiness and perfection in our application of God's Word. It is an act of aligning our personal will to God's sovereignty by transforming our minds with absolute truth and maintaining a high standard of moral integrity in our lives. It means we reject the pleasures of this world and obey God's Word instead.

The problem is that our flesh is selfish. We may have every intention of living for Jesus Christ, but when temptation comes knocking at our door, it is painstakingly difficult not to answer. When we are stressed, bored, or lonely, sin waits patiently for the opportune moment to appeal to our flesh. The enemy can sense when we are struggling to overcome difficulties and trials. That is why 1 Peter 5:8 is such an accurate picture of Satan. He prowls around waiting for us to isolate from the protection of the flock so he can devour us with relative ease, all because we choose to appease our flesh rather than honor the Lord.

Living for righteousness is not easy. Sin is pleasurable for a reason, but the instant gratification of yielding to temptation does not last. It only craves more to appease its insatiable appetite, thus demanding more fuel to keep the fire burning. That is why we desperately need deliverance from the enemy's snares to avoid plunging deeper into addiction. If only we would realize that God has already equipped us with everything we need to survive, perhaps we would not succumb to temptation so easily. For by the power of the Holy Spirit, we are free to choose whether we will yield to our flesh or live for a more honorable calling.

"Finally, brothers, whatever is true, whatever is honorable, whatever is just, whatever is pure, whatever is lovely, whatever is commendable, if there is any excellence, if there is anything worthy of praise, think about these things."

— Philippians 4:8

Righteousness is our supreme goal to conform us into the image of Jesus Christ, our perfect standard of purity and holiness (not that we could ever obtain perfection this side of heaven). Nonetheless, we strive to honor God in all we say and do, not because we are holy, but because He is worthy of our reverent praise for the sacrifice He made on the cross for us. We often forget that the same spirit who raised Jesus from the grave resides in our hearts. God has given us all we need to resist temptation. Therefore, we must obey the Spirit's conviction and stay on the straight and narrow path toward holiness.

"Worthy are you, Lord and God, to receive glory and honor and power, for you created all things, and by your will they existed and were created."

— Revelation 4:11

Righteousness flows from a river of gratitude for all Christ has done because He loves us in ways we cannot fully understand or comprehend. The blessings of God far surpass the riches of this world, for He bestows grace and favor on us every time we die to fleshly desires and respond in faith by trusting His Word. When we suffer for righteousness' sake, resisting temptation and sin, we are declaring to a lost world that we have been bought with a price. Therefore, in thanksgiving, we will devote our lives to accomplishing His sovereign will this side of heaven and pay forward to others the grace He has given us.

"I have been crucified with Christ. It is no longer I who live, but Christ who lives in me. And the life I now live in the flesh I live by faith in the Son of God, who loved me and gave himself for me."

— Galatians 2:20

That may require us to surrender all we hold dear (including our lives) and endure poverty and persecution for His name's sake. However, if we are truly Christians, we should welcome the opportunity to bear that cross because Jesus did more than we could fathom when He suffered and died to secure our eternity in heaven. The very least we can do is share the Good News of His Gospel to the nations without fear of man deterring us from His great commission. For if we will not stand for Jesus before humanity, why would we expect Him to acknowledge us before the Father on judgment day?

"And Jesus came and said to them, 'All authority in heaven and on earth has been given to me. Go therefore and make disciples of all nations, baptizing them in the name of the Father, Son, and Holy Spirit, teaching them to observe all that I have commanded you. And behold, I am with you always, to the end of the age.'"

— Matthew 28:18–20

The beauty of Psalm 34:19 is that it does not simply warn us of the impending trials and struggles we face living out our faith in Christ. Rather, it promises intervention from God during our trials to help us survive. What we typically want amid trials differs from what we need. If we are honest, we would rather avoid affliction. If there is an easier path to following Christ, we will take it, because who wants to suffer for Christ in a literal sense? However, what we need more than anything when affliction arises is to know our Savior is standing beside us in the fiery furnace, for He knows what it feels like to be persecuted for righteousness' sake.

"Then King Nebuchadnezzar was astonished and rose up in haste. He declared to his counselors, 'Did we not cast three men bound into the fire?' They answered and said to the king, 'True, O king.' He answered and said, 'But I see four men unbound, walking in the midst of the fire, and they are not hurt; and the appearance of the fourth is like a son of the gods.' Then Nebuchadnezzar came near to the door of the burning fiery furnace; he declared, 'Shadrach, Meshach, and Abednego, servants of the Most High God, come out, and come here!' Then Shadrach, Meshach, and Abednego came out from the fire."

— Daniel 3:24–26

Deliverance is not a guarantee that pain, anguish, and grief will suddenly cease if we abide in Christ. God might be encouraging us to endure persecution for His name's sake, even though the enemy wants us to believe we are hopelessly alone during our seasons of trials. That is why God guarantees deliverance from isolation and loneliness. For when we suffer for righteousness' sake, our Lord leans closer, assuring us that the sufferings of this world are temporary. He reminds us that our eternity is secure because of Christ's death, burial, and resurrection.

> *"Then Moses summoned Joshua and said to him in the sight of all Israel, 'Be strong and courageous, for you shall go with this people into the land that the LORD has sworn to their fathers to give them, and you shall put them in possession of it. It is the LORD who goes before you. He will be with you; he will not leave or forsake you. Do not fear or be dismayed.'"*

> — *Deuteronomy 31:7–8*

Remember, we are more than conquerors through Christ who strengthens us. We have everything we need to endure Satan's attacks. Victory has already been won for those who trust in Jesus Christ for eternal salvation. Therefore, if we are born-again and washed by the blood of the lamb, we are empowered to destroy strongholds by the Spirit who dwells in us. We often forget that God gave us His Spirit for wisdom, discernment, and protection. As a result, we must rely upon Him when we are struggling with spiritual warfare and need deliverance. Again, the enemy would have us believe we are all alone, but that is a lie because the Holy Spirit resides in the hearts of the redeemed.

> *"Now who is there to harm you if you are zealous for what is good? But even if you should suffer for righteousness' sake, you will be blessed. Have no fear of them, nor be troubled, but in your hearts honor Christ the Lord as holy, always being prepared to make a defense to anyone who asks you for a reason for the hope that is in you; yet do it with gentleness and respect, having a good conscience, so that, when you are slandered, those who revile your good behavior in Christ may be put to shame. For it is better to suffer for doing good, if that should be God's will, than for doing evil."*

> — *1 Peter 3:13–17*

When Jesus gave His Sermon on the Mount, He esteemed those who are persecuted for standing on the truth of Scripture. He knew the price they would pay for living counter-culturally. Therefore, when we accept Christ as our personal Lord and Savior and publicly declare we are His disciples, we place a target on our back and welcome persecution. God's Word is offensive to those who reject its authority because it is absolute truth and convicting to the soul. That is why unbelievers are unwilling to relinquish complete control of their lives to God. They refuse to submit to His supreme authority due to their pride and arrogance.

However, we should not be surprised by the affliction we receive when we defend God's Word. Rather we must embrace the opportunity to share the Gospel with those who are lost and cannot comprehend why we think and act like we do. For the day will come when we will all stand before the judgment seat of Christ and give account for our lives, which is why we must always be prepared to give ample reason for the hope we have in Jesus. We must also be willing to suffer for defending God's holy Word. Only then will we truly find rest for our weary souls till the day we see Jesus face-to-face to live forever with Him in eternity.

"If Christ be not the Substitute, He is nothing to the sinner. If He did not die as the Sin-bearer, He has died in vain... If I throw a rope to a drowning man, I am a deliverer. But is Christ no more than that? If I cast myself into the sea, and risk my life to save another, I am a deliverer. But is Christ no more? Did He but risk His life? The very essence of Christ's deliverance is the substitution of Himself for us, His life for ours. He did not come to risk His life; He came to die! He did not redeem us by a little loss, a little sacrifice, a little labor, a little suffering... He gave all He had, even His life, for us."

— *Horatius Bonar*
"God's Way of Peace," 1862.

Application

1. From whom or what do you need deliverance? How so?
2. If many are the afflictions of the righteous, why choose to live for righteousness' sake when persecution is inevitable?
3. How has God already equipped you to combat temptation? What role does the Spirit play in your heart and mind?
4. Why does righteousness flow from a river of gratitude?
5. What does it mean to bear the cross of Christ daily?
6. How can you be an ambassador for the Gospel through your pain and suffering?
7. Give an example where God stood by your side in the fiery furnace and protected you from harm. What did you learn?
8. What compels you to live counterculture as a Christ-follower?

Prayer

Lord, when I reflect upon the difficulties I have faced throughout my life, I am reminded that You have been with me in the eye of the storm more times than I can count. You have never left or forsaken me despite my foolishness. Rather, You give me comfort when I step forward in faith and am persecuted for Your name. Help me to never cower in fear of the world but stand boldly on the absolute truth of Scripture. Far too often, I forget that Your Spirit resides in my heart. When I pray for rescue from pain and suffering, I am comforted knowing that nothing I endure this side of heaven is without purpose. You are my light, my rock, and my redeemer. I surrender all to You, Lord. Amen.

The Hope of Tomorrow

Thank you for embarking on this journey of faith and unpacking twenty issues which lead to spiritual fatigue. There are far more areas of concern which could have been addressed in this book, but I pray you are encouraged to dive deep into Scripture for answers. Trials of life can easily overwhelm our minds and leave us struggling to reconcile our thoughts and emotions. Undoubtedly, Satan preys upon confusion, and many of us are so pushed to the brink that we do not know how to move forward. With that in mind, please allow me the opportunity to offer some practical advice on how to live with purpose, intentionality, and perspective moving forward.

First, begin the day with gratitude. There is something powerful about counting our blessings and giving thanks to God for His grace and mercy. I never used to do this, but I have begun lying quietly in bed when I first wake up and thanking God for a new day. If you are like me, you likely go to bed with a laundry list of things to worry about on your mind. Sometimes, I cannot sleep because my mind is constantly racing. Now, I try to begin my day on a positive note by thanking God for the opportunity to start anew with a fresh outlook on my day and the Lord as my central focus, not my problems.

Second, be on guard for spiritual attack. Sometimes, I feel like I am overthinking things by always guarding against spiritual warfare, but Satan is real and his plan is to seek and destroy. Not taking that threat seriously is a recipe for disaster, so keeping Jesus top of mind is key to survival. What that looks like is submitting and surrendering my life to God's sovereignty. If I am aligning my personal will with the Father's, I am less likely to isolate my heart and mind, because the enemy is waiting patiently for the opportune time to attack. As a result, the more I align my mind with God's Word, the less likely I am to give up, yield to sin, and surrender in defeat.

Third, consider trials with pure joy. Praising God for pruning our personal character through trials can mean the difference between spiritual growth and abandoning our faith altogether. Fire is meant to purify. So, when we face difficulty, God is giving us opportunities to grow closer to Christ. That does not mean trials are easy, but they carry purpose and meaning which we cannot see in the moment. We need hindsight perspective to find the silver-lining of God's grace amid life's storms. We will not always know why He allows trials, but we must trust that He'll reveal His reasons in due time.

Finally, rest in the arms of the Lord. More often than not, we end our days with more questions than answers. Our minds are typically exhausted from spiritual warfare we face daily. Therefore, before we succumb to mental, physical, and emotional exhaustion, we must pray and allow the Holy Spirit to convey the groanings of our hearts to God. The Lord empathizes with our weakness and knows our struggles, so there is no better place to find rest than in the shadow of the Most High. Jesus said, **"My yoke is easy and my burden is light" (Matthew 11:30)**. Therefore, we are wise to surrender our lives to Him and accept His grace by faith. That might not solve our problems today, but it will give us hope for a brighter tomorrow.

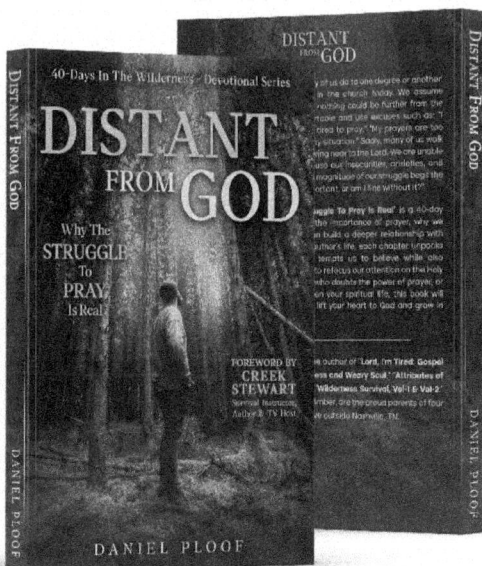

DISTANT FROM GOD
Why the Struggle to Pray is Real

Do you struggle with prayer? Many do. Praying is a common weakness in the church today. We assume everyone knows how to pray, but nothing could be further from the truth. Sadly, many of us walk away from prayer rather than drawing near to the Lord. We are unable to experience its full power because our insecurities, anxieties, and self-doubt hold us back.

"Distant From God: Why the Struggle to Pray is Real" is a 40-day devotional designed to address the importance of prayer, why we struggle to pray, and how we can build a deeper relationship with Jesus. Whether you are someone who doubts the power of prayer, or someone who is looking to deepen your spiritual life, this book will challenge and encourage you to lift your heart to God and grow in your understanding of prayer.

Target Audience: Men, Women, and Teens.

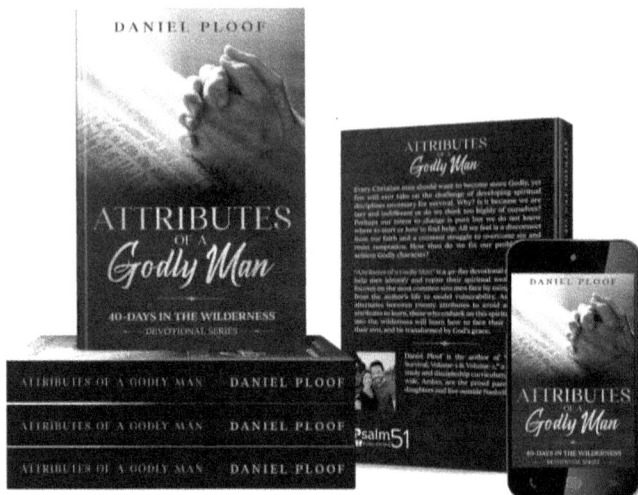

ATTRIBUTES OF A GODLY MAN

Every Christian man should want to become more Godly, yet few will ever take on the challenge of developing spiritual disciplines necessary for survival. Why? Is it because we are lazy and indifferent, or do we think too highly of ourselves? Perhaps our intent to change is pure but we do not know where to start or how to find help. All we feel is a disconnect from our faith and a constant struggle to overcome sin and resist temptation. How then do we fix our problems and achieve Godly character?

"Attributes of a Godly Man" is a 40-day devotional designed to help men identify and repair their spiritual weaknesses. It focuses on the most common sins men face daily by using examples from the author's life to model vulnerability. As each day alternates between twenty attributes to avoid and twenty attributes to learn, those who embark on this spiritual journey into the wilderness will learn how to face their fears, own their sins, and be transformed by God's grace.

Target Audience: Men, Women, and Teens.

WILDERNESS SURVIVAL
Volume-1 & Volume-2

Men's Bible Study / Discipleship Curriculum

Embark on a journey of survival training deep in the spiritual wilderness of isolation where few men dare to venture. Explore forty personal issues every man deals with in his life and marriage. Embrace the ultimate accountability challenge to become the man, husband, and father God calls you to be by transforming your life and changing your behavior.

"**Wilderness Survival**" is all about building Godly spiritual disciplines and surrendering to God's authority by examining your heart and filtering it through the absolute truth of His Word. The more you learn to guard your mind, the greater chance you will have of surviving the wilderness seasons of life and marriage, restoring the joy of your salvation, and defeating the enemy once and for all.

Target Audience: Men in relationships; preparatory for singles.

ABOUT THE AUTHOR

Daniel Ploof is the author of several Christian Living books, Bible studies, and devotionals including: **"Distant From God: Why the Struggle to Pray is Real," "Lord, I'm Tired: Gospel Truth for a Restless and Weary Soul," "Attributes of a Godly Man,"** and **"Wilderness Survival, Vol-1 & Vol-2."**

He is also the founder of **"Wilderness Survival Training,"** a resource platform designed to help Christian men and women find wisdom and discernment in God's Word. For more information and access to reflections, devotionals, and discipleship resources, please visit: **https://www.journeyintothewilderness.com**.

Daniel has been married to the love of his life and best friend, Amber, for over twenty-three years. They live outside Nashville, TN, and are the proud parents of four amazing daughters who are their greatest treasures this side of heaven.

www.ingramcontent.com/pod-product-compliance
Lightning Source LLC
Chambersburg PA
CBHW070805050426
42452CB00011B/1903